Second Edition

Teaching Our Children to Read

This book is dedicated to those teachers, researchers, educators, and leaders who have kept their common sense and are beseeching the educational community to reach an effective, working consensus on how best to teach our children to read. I hope the information provided here—which summarizes and highlights a tremendous amount of research and thinking by the leading experts in the literacy field—will help them achieve this laudable goal.

Second Edition

Teaching Our Children to Read

The Components of an Effective, Comprehensive Reading Program

Bill Honig

CORWIN PRESS, INC.
A Sage Publications Company
Thousand Oaks, California

For information:

Corwin Press, Inc.
A Sage Publications Company
2455 Teller Road
Thousand Oaks, California 91320
E-mail: order@corwinpress.com

Sage Publications Ltd.
6 Bonhill Street
London EC2A 4PU
United Kingdom

Sage Publications India Pvt. Ltd.
M-32 Market
Greater Kailash I
New Delhi 110 048 India

Printed in the United States of America

Library of Congress Cataloging-in-Publication Data

Honig, Bill.
    Teaching our children to read: The components of an effective, comprehensive reading program / by Bill Honig.— 2nd ed.
  p. cm.
    Includes bibliographical references and index.
 ISBN 0-7619-7529-2 (cloth: acid-free paper)
 ISBN 0-7619-7530-6 (pbk.: acid-free paper)
  1. Reading. 2. Reading (Elementary) I. Title.
  LB1050 .H64 2000
  372.4—dc21

                                         00-010335

This book is printed on acid-free paper.

01 02 03 04 05 06 10 9 8 7 6 5 4 3 2 1

Production Editor:	Denise Santoyo
Editorial Assistant:	Cindy Bear
Typesetter/Designer:	Rebecca Evans/Barbara Burkholder
Indexer:	Pamela Van Huss

Contents

Preface to the Second Edition

When I wrote the first edition of this book, there was a great deal of controversy about the role of direct skill instruction in teaching children to read. In the past 5 years, scientific research and studies of effective teaching practices have quelled the controversy. Today, except for a few holdouts, there is general consensus that in addition to varied language-based and literature-based activities, reading instruction should include explicit and systematic instruction in the basic skills that help students become fluent, automatic readers. Across the country, policy makers, educators, and publishers have begun to respond. The real challenge is how to implement what we know are the best research-based practices in adopting reading materials, in training teachers, and in school leadership.

I cofounded the Coalition on Reading (CORE) to help educators meet this challenge. Since 1995, CORE has worked collaboratively with schools and districts, committed to the goal of helping *all* students learn to read. To date, CORE has trained more than 17,000 educators in 600 schools and 70 school districts throughout the western states. We have seen significant results. In California, for example, in 2000, CORE trained the teachers of more than 18,000 second grade students. These students gained an average of 13 percentile points on the SAT-9 test from 1998 to 2000—approximately 50% more than the gain experienced in the rest of the state. When effective materials and competent leadership were present, the CORE schools did even better. Similar results have been achieved in CORE schools in other states and in non-CORE projects, such as those in Inglewood and Sacramento, California, and in Fort Worth, Texas, where schools have implemented a systematic, explicit program of sequenced skills development in reading.

This second edition has grown out of the experiences of scores of dedicated teachers and their success in the classroom. It provides an updated overview of important research and instructional strategies that will bring all students to higher levels of literacy. Expanded sections on phonics instruction; connected practice with decodable text; fluency; multisyllabic word instruction; spelling; vocabulary and concept development; strategic reading; text organization; book discussions; and literacy benchmarks, assessment, and intervention are included. New tables with sound/spelling correspondences and percentages are provided in Resource A. There are also revisions to the major points discussed in Resource B.

For more information about proven practices in the teaching of reading, please refer to the CORE Literacy Series: *CORE Teaching Reading Sourcebook* (Honig, Diamond, & Gutlohn, 2000), *CORE Assessing Reading* (CORE, 2000), and *CORE Reading Research Anthology* (CORE, 1999b).

Acknowledgments

I want to thank Jacalyn Mahler whose special talent in understanding reading and able editing made this revision possible, the CORE staff for its tireless efforts to improve reading instruction, the CORE Advisory Board, and those teachers and administrators who have used the research discussed in this book to help countless students learn to read.

—Bill Honig

About the Author

Bill Honig is the cofounder and president of CORE, a professional development organization that has helped thousands of educators successfully implement comprehensive, research-based literacy programs. From 1983 to 1993, he was California State Superintendent of Public Instruction. Under his leadership, the State Department of Education issued nationally renowned frameworks in each of the disciplines. During his tenure as Visiting Distinguished Professor at San Francisco State University, he served as director of the Center for Systemic School Reform.

Bill Honig is coauthor of *CORE: Teaching Reading Sourcebook,* which is part of the CORE Literacy Series. He is also the author of *Last Chance for Our Children: How You Can Help Save Our Schools* (1985) and the *Handbook for Planning an Effective Reading Program* (1979). In addition to these titles, he has written numerous articles and been the recipient of several prestigious awards.

1

The Case for a
Balanced Approach

The first and foremost job of elementary school is to teach children to read. The reading program in every school should enable almost every student to be able to read fluently and understand grade-appropriate material by the end of elementary school; to have read a large number of books, magazines, and other informational text; to reach high levels of comprehension ability; and to enjoy and learn from reading. These goals can be achieved only if most students are able to decode and read beginning material by the mid-first grade and have perfected these basic skills to tackle more difficult texts by third grade. Most students who fail to learn to read by this time are destined to fall farther and farther behind in school and are effectively prevented from capitalizing on the power of education to improve and enrich their lives (Juel 1988, 1994; Stanovich 1986, 1993b). Yet large numbers of students do not become readers early enough to develop the skills and experience to read age-appropriate materials throughout their elementary careers and are, in effect, excluded from instruction.

Access to further education, high-skilled jobs, and a chance to participate fully as informed citizens depends in large part on school success, which itself is highly correlated with the ability to read. Given what is known today about the techniques of teaching youngsters to read, no reason exists for this potentially dangerous state of affairs. Reading failure is preventable.

Educators must examine current reading practices critically; identify the most successful programs and approaches; and enlist teachers, parents, and leaders responsible for educating our children in the common goal of remedying this unnecessary situation.

The Great Debate

Five years ago, controversy and confusion in the literacy field centered around how best to teach children to read. Specifically, the question was, Should skills be taught directly in an organized and explicit skills development program as part of beginning-to-read instruction, or will students acquire these skills more indirectly by being read to, immersion in print, and learning them in the context of reading for meaning—an approach known as *whole language?*

Research by leading experts in the field of literacy has shown that it is not an either-or question. The most effective reading instruction uses a balanced and comprehensive approach that includes the explicit, systematic teaching of phonemic awareness and phonics as well as an abundance of rich and varied literature and writing practice (Adams, 1990, 1991; Adams & Bruck, 1995; Beck & Juel, 1995; National Reading Panel, 2000; Pressley, Rankin, & Yokoi, 1996; Share & Stanovich, 1995b; Snow, Burns, & Griffin, 1998; Stahl, 1992; Wharton-McDonald & Pressley, 1998). It is now conventional wisdom that only through direct skill instruction can all children learn to automatically recognize a growing number of words and possess the necessary tools to decipher new words they encounter. (The 24 major points made in this book about the role of skills in a comprehensive elementary reading program are summarized in Resource A.)

More than 30 years ago, Jeanne Chall exhaustively reviewed the research on beginning-reading programs in her classic 1967 study, *Learning to Read: The Great Debate* (see also Chall, 1983, 1992, 1995). She concluded that beginning-reading programs that emphasized decoding or phonics, the direct and systematic focus on the system that maps print to speech, and the opportunity to practice learning that system in the context of reading were much more effective than those that solely used meaning-based approaches. This is because thoroughly decoding a word builds the sound/pattern and meaning connections that enable readers to automatically recognize the word on subsequent readings.

Dr. Reid Lyon, head of reading research at the National Institute of Child Health and Human Development, has said that there is no debate—at a certain stage of reading, phonics is necessary. Then, children need literature to read. Teachers' classroom routines should include reading good literature to students and discussing it with them, especially by asking questions that stretch children's minds beyond the literal meaning of the text. Teachers should fill the classroom with a wide variety of high-quality materials and create a literate environment. Students should have a multitude of opportunities to read along with the teacher, work together on reading and writing activities, write daily, and dictate stories about their interests. Teachers should give students choices in their reading, help them to relate what they know to what they are going to read, assist them in keeping reading logs, and offer them the chance to respond personally to what they have read. (For a summary of classroom activities and organizational strategies to incorporate these ideas, see Depree & Iversen, 1994; for a summary of these techniques, see Smith, 1982.)

The whole-language movement has improved classrooms by promoting practices that encourage students to read outstanding literature, including both fiction and, more recently, quality nonfiction; write more; and perceive writing as having a purpose and communicating something important (Pressley & Rankin, 1994, p. 59).

At one time, the crucial issue in reading instruction was whether there *also* should be an organized and directly taught, explicit skills development component that stresses decoding words and learning the sound/symbol system. Some people have argued against the inclusion of explicit skills development instruction, claiming that explicit instruction is unnecessary and even harmful. These objections are without merit.

Objection #1: Children Learn to Read "Naturally"

Some natural learning advocates contend that children will either intuit how print maps to sound or recognize the meaning of the word by other methods, such as guessing its meaning from the context or shape, and that teachers can fill in skills gaps when they arise.

Unfortunately, these claims have proven false for a significant number of children. In a comprehensive review, two top educational researchers,

David Share and Keith Stanovich (1995b), surveyed the vast scientific and educational literature and concluded that all these assumptions have been conclusively refuted: guessing from context is not an effective way of learning to read, reading is not acquired naturally in the same way as speech,[1] and analyzing and learning to abstract parts of words does not hinder learning to read—it is indispensable (Foorman, 1995; Share & Stanovich, 1995b, pp. 3, 30, 32). Foorman (1995) and Share and Stanovich (1995b) cite numerous studies that have shown that (a) the primary and most efficient strategy for unlocking the meaning of a word is to visually process the letters of that word and that weak readers who cannot decode efficiently tend to overrely on context and (b) guessing an unrecognized word from context clues is an ineffective decoding strategy because it is successful only 10% to 25% of the time with content words. Note that the relative effectiveness of using context as the primary method to recognize words, decode new words, and become automatic with words is a different question than whether the use of context accelerates word recognition with accomplished readers. It does (see also Biemiller, 1994).[2]

In fact, studies by Dale Willows (Morgan & Willows, 1998) in Toronto have shown that even English language learners with limited oral vocabularies benefit from early decoding instruction. These students did just as well as English speakers who received explicit instruction in phonemic awareness and phonics, and they significantly outperformed English speakers who did not receive such instruction. The English language learners who did not receive skill instruction, however, lagged far behind the other three groups. Thus, without systematic instruction in the sound structure system of English and letter/sound correspondences, these students are especially vulnerable to reading failure. When teaching decoding to English language learners, teachers must make sure that students understand the meanings of the words they are decoding because automatic recognition requires readers to retrieve letter pattern, sound, and meaning information.

Moreover, the belief that almost all students can learn to read without an organized, explicit skill strand has taken root in too many schools and districts with disastrous results. Due to the absence of early, organized skill instruction, a large number of students are still not reaching their optimal levels of reading proficiency. A significant number of students in many high-poverty areas are remaining, in effect, nonreaders, and significantly more than 50% of students in these areas are not becoming fluent readers of grade-appropriate materials (Torgesen, Wagner, & Rashotte, 1994). When these students attempt to study for their lessons in later grades, they will stumble over many words that will prevent them from attending to meaning. Consequently, they will be unable to participate in grade-level instruction and will fall farther and farther behind during their school careers.

Most of these children will have been barred from becoming fluent readers of grade-level text because they did not receive an organized skills strand early enough to become independent readers of beginning materials in first grade and thus read enough books successfully to stay on track (Liberman, Shankweiler, & Liberman, 1991; Stanovich 1986, 1993b). In *Listening to Children Read Aloud: Data From NAEP's Integrated Reading Performance Record (IRPR) at Grade 4,* Pinnell et al. (1995), for example, found that large numbers of fourth graders had very low fluency and reading rates, with reading rates dropping compared to previous years (pp. 21-23, 40-42). If students are not independently reading beginning materials by mid-first grade, they have only a slim chance of reading at grade level by third grade and beyond, unless they receive an extraordinary tutoring program (Juel, 1994, p. 125).

Studies have revealed several factors that put children at special risk for reading failure: poverty, phonological processing and memory difficulties, speech and hearing impairments, language barriers, and parents' low reading abilities (Lyon, 1998). Respected educator Lisa Delpit (1995) has noted repeatedly that children from lower socioeconomic families, primarily clustered in urban areas, are especially harmed by the absence of a structured phonics and skills program. Similarly, students with some auditory or memory processing problems—found in all schools and estimated to be as many as 20% of all children—are also especially harmed if a skills strand is missing. For these students, learning to read is a powerful equity issue.

The large subpopulation of students with dyslexia, most of whom are unidentified and situated in regular classrooms, has been extensively studied (Adams, 1990; Berninger, 1997; Hall & Moats, 1999; Liberman et al., 1991; Lyon, 1994, 1995; Moats, 1994; Shaywitz, 1996).[3] According to the research, most of the students who *are* designated as *learning* disabled and become identified as special education students are really *reading* and *spelling* disabled. They have difficulty breaking the symbol/sound code of the language. Yet had they received appropriate instruction in kindergarten and first grade, many of these students would not be in special education. In addition, many of the students who have difficulty learning to read but who are never identified as learning disabled suffer from the same phonological processing difficulties.

The main problem for both these groups of students is an inability to recognize, manipulate, and learn the distinct sounds of spoken language (phonemes) and how these sounds correspond to letters and letter patterns in printed text. Lack of phonemic awareness is the most powerful predictor of difficulty in learning to read. Without it, students have an extremely difficult time learning how to use phonics skills to read through a word, generate the sounds the letters represent, and connect the pronunciation with a meaningful word. Unfortunately, many teachers and school policymakers do not understand that a large proportion of their students who are struggling to learn to read are actually suffering from specific phonological processing difficulties or a lack of phonics knowledge that prevent them from learning the sound/symbol system and using phonics and other word attack skills. Consequently, many schools fail to provide these students with timely instructional intervention, and as a result, most of these students will fall significantly and irrevocably behind in reading—*a preventable mishap for all but a few.* Researchers estimate that all but 3% to 5% of children can learn to read with direct instruction in phonemic awareness and phonics (Lyon, 1998; Torgesen et al., 1994). The remaining students require intensive support, such as Phonological Awareness Training (Torgesen & Bryant, 1994), which includes auditory practice with both discriminating and articulating distinct speech sounds. Another barrier to timely intervention is the prevailing erroneous opinion that many students in the early grades are not developmentally ready for reading instruction and will "grow out" of their problems with the passage of time.[4,5]

Even the 60% to 70% of children who come to school already supported by rich literary experiences, and who eventually will learn to read under any instructional system or philosophy, need supportive skills instruction. Because teachers don't know precisely which students will be among the 60% to 70%, it makes sense to provide *all* students with direct instruction in the alphabetic system. Explicit, systematic instruction will accelerate and consolidate all students' learning. Without this support, many will end up reading significantly below their potential in later grades for the following reasons adapted from Adams (1990):

- These children need to review the symbol/sound relationships they have already encountered.
- They need to develop that fragmented knowledge into a systematic understanding of the entire letter/sound system so that they learn how to learn new words by themselves, without having to

rely on memorizing them. Children encounter two kinds of new words. They must learn how to read and become fluent with words they have not yet seen in print but which are in their speaking or listening vocabulary. They also must learn how to read and infer the meaning of words not yet in their *spoken* vocabulary—words they will encounter with increasing frequency in the later grades— or many will start to falter in subsequent years.

※ All students must be continually monitored to assure they are making progress, reading books at the right level for learning, and not suffering from any gaps in their knowledge. Teachers can best accomplish this by taking observational notes while the student reads.

※ Children need to learn the skills beyond phonics, phonemic awareness, and word attack strategies, which extend reading. These include spelling, grammar, word and language structures, and mechanics. (p. 283)

In summary, for these children to reach their reading potential in the later grades, early, direct assistance in alphabet recognition; print concepts; phonemic awareness; phonics; high-frequency words; and recognition of word parts, such as syllables, affixes, base words, and phonograms, must be provided.

Objection #2: Organized, Explicit Phonics Programs Result in Rigid Pedagogy

It is true that all too often, phonics is taught outside the context of reading. Children are given a series of "rules" and then spend their time circling and coloring pictures on work sheets. The problem is compounded by the fact that in the past, many published phonics programs did not provide appropriate reading materials. The stories children were expected to read contained few words with the letter/sound correspondences they had been taught during the phonics lesson and few words that were decodable based on what they had been taught in previous lessons (Stein, Johnson, & Gutlohn, 1999). This means that students had few opportunities to practice and build on the particular skills they were learning. Blevins (1998) explains in his commendable summary of phonics instruction, *Phonics from A to Z:* "If this happens, children are likely to undervalue the importance of the phonics they're learning. Why should they pay attention during phonics lessons when they rarely use what they learn?"

Major research studies have shown the benefits of systematic, explicit phonics instruction in early grades (Adams, 1990; Beck & Juel, 1995; Chall, 1996; Chall & Popp, 1996). The key is implementing well-designed instruction. To be effective, instruction must be sequential and tailored to students' specific needs. It must actively engage them by building on their understanding of how language works, helping them identify sound/spelling correspondences in isolation, blending these sounds into recognizable words, and applying all that they have learned to reading connected text. The importance of practice with decodable text cannot be overstated because it is by successfully reading text that students are able to increase their fluency and automaticity. Dictation and spelling and word work activities also play key roles in effective phonics instruction. Dictation and spelling activities show students how they can use their sound/spelling knowledge to communicate through writing. Word work— building, manipulating, and sorting words—gives students hands-on practice that reinforces their understanding of sound/spelling patterns (Honig, Diamond, & Gutlohn, 2000).

It is important to understand the proper place and scope of phonics instruction. Although there are hundreds of different spellings for the 42 to 44 phonemes in the English language, it is only necessary to teach the most useful ones—approximately 100. Instruction in these letter/sound correspondences and in high-frequency words should be completed at the end of first, or the beginning of second grade, allowing students to tackle text and learn more about the letter/sound system of English through self-teaching or targeted, individualized instruction (or both). The goal is to get students reading authentic texts, such as fiction and nonfiction trade books, poetry, and magazines, as soon as possible. Systematic, sequential phonics instruction is the best way to get them off to a fast start.

Objection #3: English Is Too Irregular to Make Phonics Instruction Worthwhile

Although English spelling is complex, it is also orderly and patterned (Chomsky & Halle, 1968; Taylor, 1981; Venezky, 1970). According to a report published by the U.S. Office of Education (Hanna, Hanna, Hodges, & Rudorf, 1966), at least 20 English phonemes have spellings that are over 90% predictable, and 10 others are predictable more than

80% of the time. The study also found that approximately 50% of all English words are completely regular (spelled with letters and letter patterns that represent their most common sounds, e.g., *had*). An additional 37% of words are off by only one sound (e.g., *put*).

Successful Early Reading Programs in Practice

The most effective teachers are *already* using the best practices proposed by the advocates of a balanced approach.

Researchers have examined the practices of teachers who have had exceptional success in teaching children to read (Pressley & Rankin, 1994; Pressley et al., 1996). Regardless of whether the teachers characterized themselves as "whole-language" or "skills-based," they all used an approach that combined a rich array of the language-based and literature-based activities with comprehensive, explicit skill instruction. These effective teachers provide direct instruction in the following:

- Alphabet recognition—visually recognizing and naming the letters of the alphabet
- Phonemic awareness—understanding that spoken language is composed of individual sounds, or phonemes, and orally blending, segmenting, and manipulating those sounds
- The alphabetic principle—understanding that letters of the alphabet, either singly or in combination, represent the sounds of spoken language
- Phonics—the study and use of sound/spelling correspondences to help identify written words
- Decoding—converting a printed word into its spoken form by connecting letter patterns with sounds
- Other word attack skills—automatic recognition of high-frequency words, breaking words into smaller parts (syllables, affixes, base words, and phonograms), and use of context to confirm pronunciation and resolve ambiguity

For the most part, these experienced professionals teach these skills by having students read appropriate materials, but they also teach the skills in isolation, usually in relatively small blocks of time, in a problem-solving, active manner with the aim of giving students conscious control of the sound/symbol system. Direct instruction is especially effective for weaker readers and students in special education. These excellent teachers are able to use and integrate a number of complicated instructional strategies to tailor effective approaches to meet the diverse needs of their students. It has taken most of them years of effort, study, and commitment to reach this level of effectiveness.

Essential Components of an Effective Literacy Program

During the past two decades, cognitive scientists and the country's top reading experts have corroborated the effectiveness of what our best practitioners have been doing all along. Their research has produced a much clearer picture of the essential components and instructional strategies of an effective early literacy program.

The consensus of these reading experts is that an effective literacy program for all children must include *both* a multitude of print and language-rich (whole language) activities, such as reading to children, discussing stories, and writing frequently, *and* explicit, organized, and systematic skills development.

These top experts agree that the goals of any early reading program should be to enable almost every student to comprehend and read fluently grade-appropriate material, understand the meaning of what they have read, be well-read, and enjoy and be able to learn from reading.

These specialists also maintain that these goals can be accomplished only if most students are independently reading beginning books by mid-first grade (or the equivalent in ungraded primaries).

To become independent readers, children first need the basic tools to break the code of written English. They need to be able hear and manipulate the sounds in spoken words, visually recognize letters, connect letter patterns with their corresponding sounds, and be able to apply all of this knowledge when they encounter a new word in text. It is especially important for students to understand the system of letter/sound correspondences well enough to generate possible alternative pronunciations for given letter patterns and to then use the meaning of the passage as a whole to confirm the pronunciation and resolve any ambiguity. (A listing of common consonant and vowel sound/spellings appears in Resource A.) This is what occurs with the first reading of a word like *bread,* which contains a vowel pair that can have a long-*a* (*steak*), long-*e* (*bead*), or short-*e* sound (*head*). Students also need abundant opportunities to practice these skills with manageable texts, word play, and writing activities.

This skills development strand should be *sequenced and adjusted individually* if a student already knows the skill, *and* it must include *large amounts of practice,* both to develop automaticity with a growing number of words and to become more adept at decoding new words, until the use of these skills becomes automatic. Automatic and accurate recognition of individual words leads to the fluent reading of strings of words, which in turn leads to full comprehension—the goal of reading. When readers struggle over individual words, they aren't able remember or synthesize the information presented in the text. That is why it is so important that good teaching practices in the early grades lay the foundation for later fluency.

Skills should be taught *explicitly and directly,* not as rote learning but in an *active, thinking, problem-solving way* (children as "word detectives"), with the reading of interesting stories and nonfiction materials as the medium for learning to use and think about these skills. This can be accomplished by reading with the teacher, reading with a classmate or a parent, reading along with a taped version of the story, or just by reading independently. Initially, these materials should be either specifically designed or appropriate to reinforce the skills being learned.

Last, the experts recommend that for students to become readers by late first grade, the following sequence of benchmarks and instruction should be adopted:

1. Students must leave *kindergarten* knowing letter names, shapes, some letter sounds, and high-frequency words; possessing basic phonemic, syntactic, and print awareness; and having listening, discussion, and oral telling and retelling skills.
2. *By mid-first grade,* students should be able to sound out simple consonant/vowel/consonant (CVC) words with short vowels, consonant digraphs and blends, and words with long-vowel patterns. To do this, they must have more advanced phonemic and syntactic awareness, a solid grasp of the basic sound/symbol system, and repeated practice blending sounds into recognizable words. Writing and word work activities reinforce students' knowledge of how print maps to sound. By the end of first grade, students should be able to automatically recognize 150 plus words (including those that are fully decodable) of the 300 words that occur most frequently in print[6] and read single-syllable words with high-

utility vowel digraphs, *r*-controlled vowels, and common phonograms. They should also begin to read longer words using new
word attack strategies, such as breaking compound words into
two base words and reading the inflectional endings -*ing* and -*es* as
chunks.

Thus, by mid-first grade, most children should have learned the critical mass of skills that enable them to begin reading books or anthologies,
including both literature and nonfiction at appropriate levels of difficulty.
These materials then become the vehicle to learn and apply the skills being
taught in specific lessons. By this stage, many students should be increasingly able to teach themselves and learn the rest of the letter/sound system
by reading large amounts of material. These independent learners still
should be taught more advanced decoding skills, be taught to recognize an
increasing number of words automatically by reading specific words successfully several times, and be monitored for progress and gaps in learning
by the teacher. However, many children who have auditory or visual processing problems or who have very little exposure to reading and reading
materials will need more structured lessons in these beginning-reading
techniques well into the second and third grades.

Consequently, from mid-first grade on, a balanced program should
extend reading power. It should provide *extensive opportunities for students to read varied books and materials;* offer explicit instruction in comprehension and oral language development; and teach other skills strands,
such as spelling, the more complex syllabication patterns, word and language structure, grammar, composition, vocabulary, the text organization
of narrative and expository text, strategic reading, independent reading,
and book discussions.

*If schools follow these guidelines, almost every child should become a
strong reader.*

Comprehensive and Balanced:
Not the Same as Eclectic

Contrary to what some critics may think, a balanced approach does
not mean a mushy eclecticism. Beginning-to-read strategies must incorporate a set of strands that is comprehensive enough to ensure that all
children will read. Within this set, each strand must be designed according

to best practices and be thoughtfully integrated and reinforced by other strands.

However, these decoding skill-strands must not become so jumbled with other strands that students miss the point, as is currently the case with much classroom instruction that stresses integrated language arts activities and attempts to deal with skills on the fly or haphazardly. Nor should skills be taught in such an isolated and rote manner that students fail to connect skill understanding with the actual practice of reading.

These beginning-to-read strategies are consistent with the current standards of several states and national institutions, which call for students to be

* Fluent readers by the third grade
* Well-read
* Able to understand grade-level materials
* Able to apply their writing skills to organize information
* Able to argue a point, tell a story, and respond to a literary or nonfiction piece
* Able to participate in an ongoing conversation or make a more formal presentation to the class
* Proficient in spelling, grammar, and language mechanics
* Able to effectively discuss the ideas contained in literature or nonfiction

Summary

According to the overwhelming consensus of the best practitioners and top researchers, an effective reading program should be integrated with the other language arts, such as writing, speaking, and listening. High-quality early literacy programs should create a print-rich and language-rich environment through reading aloud to students and discussing literature and nonfiction with children, a strong independent-reading strand based on the availability of good children's literature, writing to communicate, and many shared reading activities.

However, because these instructional strategies are, by themselves, not enough to teach many children to read well, specific skills development components also must be included, such as print concepts, alphabet recognition, phonemic awareness, phonics, word structure, and word attack and self-monitoring skills. In addition, these skills must be taught in an organized and systematic manner at the beginning of any reading program if all children are going to learn to read. Students should be taught these skills in an active, problem-solving manner that offers plenty of opportunities to practice the skills in actual reading and writing situations.

Chapters 3 through 8 address the recommended specific components of an organized skills program, when these skills should be taught, and how they should be taught.

Notes

1. For a penetrating attack on this naturalistic fallacy, see Pressley and Rankin (1994, pp. 160-161). These authors find that the original research done by Chomsky, who assumed that oral-language syntactical competence cannot be taught, has not held up. Most special education programs now do successfully teach language structure. In addition, the mental processes used for reading, such as visual processing, visual discrimination, visual short-term memory, and phonological awareness, evolved in humans for very different purposes than reading and writing and need assistance to be converted to the complicated task of deciphering print, whereas a case can be made that oral processing abilities did evolve to assist humans in understanding and producing speech and operate much more automatically.

2. For an excellent explanation of how the ability to learn to speak depends on the recognition of deep patterns that are biologically hard-wired in our brains (in contrast to learning to read), see Steven Pinker's (1994) best-seller, *The Language Instinct: How the Mind Creates Language*.

3. Some of the most comprehensive research on this issue that supports the necessity for a structured skills component has been directed and sponsored by Dr. G. Reid Lyon of the National Institute of Child, Health, and Human Development in Bethesda, Maryland. This institute has invested more than $80 million in large-scale research projects and longitudinal studies of children during the past several years to ascertain the causes of learning disabilities and to determine if the consensus position on a balanced approach to teaching beginning reading is correct. This research is described by Lyon in *Research in Learning Disabilities at the NICHD* (1994) and "Research Initiatives in Learning Disabilities" (1995). The former document cites findings from the sponsored research projects that have studied these issues and conducted intensive longitudinal studies of large numbers of students from early childhood to high school. Some of their findings:

> Reading disabled or dyslexic children comprise 20% of students, and three quarters of third-grade students who are reading disabled will remain disabled in the ninth grade. (p. 10)

> Disabled readers do not readily acquire the alphabetic code when learning to read due to deficiencies in phonological processing. As such, dis-

abled readers must be presented highly structured, explicit and intensive instruction in phonics rules and the application of the rules to print. (p. 12)

The ability to read and comprehend depends upon rapid and automatic recognition and decoding of single words, and slow and inaccurate decoding are the best predictors of difficulty in reading comprehension. (p. 11)

The ability to decode single words accurately and fluently is dependent upon the ability to segment words and syllables into abstract constituent sound units (phonemes). Deficits in phonological awareness reflect the core deficit in dyslexia. (p. 10)

The best predictor of reading ability/disability from kindergarten and first grade test performance is phoneme segmentation ability. (p. 11)

Longitudinal data indicate that systematic structured phonics instruction results in more favorable outcomes in reading than does a context-emphasis (whole language) approach. (p. 12)

4. Studies support the compelling need for an approach that combines skills and whole-language techniques for special education students. These include Michael Pressley and Joan Rankin's (1994) *More About Whole Language Methods of Reading Instruction for Students at Risk for Early Reading Failure.*

5. Lyon (1995) writes that "[r]eading disability reflects a persistent deficit rather than a development lag in linguistic and reading skills [citations omitted]" (p. 10). Resistance to early instruction in preschool, kindergarten, and early first grade sometimes stems from a confusion of two meanings of "developmentally appropriate." The more hard-line *maturational* approach states that students are not ready for instruction and need "the gift of time." Lyon's research and other studies demonstrate that only a very small number of students cannot master the skills being discussed for kindergarten and first grade, such as letter recognition, sound blending, and beginning phonics. It is not "developmentally appropriate" to wait. A more realistic *interventionist* approach maintains that organized instructional support (which can be gamelike) at the appropriate time is beneficial. The research cited earlier goes further and finds that intervention is essential. For most students at risk of not learning to read, the failure to intervene early means they will never become proficient readers.

6. The Dolch Basic Sight Vocabulary (Dolch, 1955) and Instant Words (Fry, 1994) are two examples of high-frequency word lists—the words that appear most frequently in primary reading texts.

2

What Skilled Readers Do

What is it about learning to read that makes being able to hear and distinguish the individual sounds of words, decoding, and word attack so important? To understand the importance of these skills to beginning readers, it is first necessary to examine the nature of *skilled* reading and then a different and more complex issue—the process of learning to read.

Reading is about constructing meaning from text. Good readers begin with attention to individual words and then string these words together into a meaningful whole. Thus, there are two major sources of meaning: words and passages. Proficient readers recognize individual words and retrieve their meaning rapidly, effortlessly, and unconsciously. This automatic word recognition frees their minds to focus on the more complex task of extracting meaning from the entire passage, which is an active, conscious process. Passage understanding involves grouping words into phrases, weaving sentences together, thinking about the author's message or main ideas, and drawing on prior knowledge about the topic and text structure.

The Importance of Seeing
Letter Combinations in Words

The key to unlocking meaning starts with the automatic recognition of each written word, which brings the meaning of that word to consciousness. Proficient readers visually process a word and search their long-term memory for a word that matches its letters and letter patterns. This is done extremely rapidly and effortlessly, drawing on their stored knowledge of letter/sound correspondences, word meaning, text structure, and syntax. Thoroughly decoding a word the first few times gives the reader connected sound, symbol, and meaning information and establishes the necessary neural connections in the brain. Reading the word successfully a number of times strengthens the connections and speeds up the retrieval process.

The automatic recognition of words frees a student's mind to concentrate on the meaning of the word in relation to its phrase, the sentence, and the story. For proficient readers, automatic recognition takes place swiftly, effortlessly, and unconsciously, and uses a minimum of working memory capacity, allowing the reader to concentrate on the meaning of the passage (Adams, 1990, pp. 107-135; Juel, 1994, pp. 1-2). Share and Stanovich (1995b) write that

> There is no known teaching method that has resulted in good reading comprehension without simultaneously leading to the development of at least adequate word recognition ability. Furthermore, an overwhelming amount of evidence indicates that the proximal impediment to reading in at-risk and reading-disabled children is difficulty in recognizing words [citations omitted]. (p. 3)

The Importance of Connecting Letter
Combinations With Discrete Sounds and Meaning

Researchers strongly insist that recoding, or connecting the letter patterns to the word's sounds, is an essential step the first times a word is read, until the spelling pathways are established in the mind. That is why decoding ability and phonemic awareness are so essential in learning to read. Using MRI technology, scientists have been able to map the parts of the brain used to read (Shaywitz, 1996). They discovered that three different areas of the brain are involved. Information about visual patterns (letters, letter combinations, syllables) is stored in one area. Information about the sounds associated with those patterns is stored in another area, and information about meaning is stored in a third area. Contrary to long-held beliefs, reading is not a purely visual process. After the eye scans the printed letters in a word, the brain matches each letter pattern to discrete sounds. The bundled sound/symbol information is then connected to the meaning of the word in the context of the particular chunk of text.

This "chunking" facilitates retention of the meaning of strings of words in the reader's mind. At the same time, it provides the reader with hints about whether any of the potential word candidates being generated from memory by the letter and sound clues make sense in relation to the meaning of what is being read (Adams, 1990).[1]

All three mental systems interact with each other as often as necessary to narrow down the candidate words stored in memory that could possibly match the letter patterns and potential associated sounds while also being consistent with the meaning of the passage, until the exact appropriate match is found and becomes conscious. The entire process is automatic, unconscious, extremely rapid, and perceived by the accomplished reader as effortless. The reader is busy attending to the meaning of the word just retrieved in relation to other words and phrases that have already been read.

There have been several widespread misconceptions about how skilled readers actually read. For example, it was once commonly believed that skilled readers do not need to read letters or even words because that would slow them down. But according to extensive eye movement research (Kolers, 1976), even accomplished readers *do look at virtually every word, although they sometimes skip short function words, such as* and, to, the, *or* of. They also accurately perceive every letter in each word, not linearly but in chunks (Adams, 1990, pp. 100-102). They do this so rapidly—averaging five words or more per second—that they can recognize phrases and words at almost the same time they recognize individual letters.

This seeming paradox can be explained. Skilled readers, although they perceive every letter, do not need to see each one independently; rather, they can simultaneously search both the print and their long-term memories for matching patterns. Thus, they look at letters in combination, and because they have so much prior experience with the variety of high-frequency letter or spelling patterns in words and how words are broken into syllables, they can quickly use this knowledge to narrow down the possibilities and find the word that exactly fits a particular pattern (Adams, 1990, pp. 108-115).

Readers depend on a combination of information about a word's visual pattern, its possible sounds, and its meaning. Partial storage of only the first and last letters of a word, or only the letters without the sounds, doesn't give the brain enough information to store or retrieve efficiently. That is why readers who do not thoroughly sound out or analyze words alphabetically when they first encounter them continue to struggle. They only have one mental system operating. For the neural connections to be strong enough for automaticity, students have to read the word successfully a number of times.

Thus, it is apparent why another misconception about reading is detrimental. Beginning readers who rely too heavily on contextual clues, such as pictures or the connection of other words in the passage, are distracted from looking at the letters in a word and connecting those letter patterns to words in their minds. Contextual and structural clues do accelerate reading in proficient readers but cannot replace looking at letter patterns to initiate the mental search for a word. Even in the case of irregular words, readers visually scan through them, connect all the sounds (expected and unexpected) to the letters or letter combinations, and then consolidate their recognition by reading the words successfully several times (Gough & Walsh, 1991; Lovett, 1987; Treiman & Baron, 1981). For this reason, it is important when teaching irregular words to use techniques such as a spell-out strategy and sounding out with contextual analysis so that students have to attend to all of the letters. According to Andrew Biemiller (1994), a noted researcher from the University of Toronto, proficient sixth-grade readers can recognize words about .20 to .25 seconds faster if words are read in context rather than out of context, effectively doubling their reading speed from approximately ½ second a word to ¼ second a word, or 240 words per minute. Biemiller is also critical of claims that children can learn to read relying on context clues without learning the alphabetic principle and the sound/spelling system. Moreover, Biemiller underscores that becoming proficient in reading requires decoding ability and that even proficient readers revert to sounding out when confronted with difficult material or with words they do not know. Logically, then, readers should be encouraged to try to read every word and to look at the letters in each word if they wish to read fluently. Even when students ask for assistance with a word, they should subsequently try to read it (pp. 203-209).

Reliance on contextual clues is a technique usually used by readers with poor decoding skills and correlates with low reading performance (Share & Stanovich, 1995b, pp. 5-6). Conversely, word calling—saying the word without apparent understanding of meaning—can be evidence of weak vocabulary or syntactical understanding, because these are also associated with low reading levels (Pinnell et al., 1995, p. 22). However, often what appears to be word calling is, in fact, a slowing down caused by weak decoding skills and difficult material (Share & Stanovich, 1995b).[2]

Skills Needed to Become a Proficient Reader

Research showing what good readers do helps focus the discussion but does not necessarily answer the question of how a person *becomes* a skilled reader—that is a different story. For example, knowing how to sound out a word may be essential as a way station to effortless recognition of that word; phonics helps a student read a new word or place that word in long-term memory by forcing the mind to attend to spelling and sound patterns. However, sounding out words is a very slow and cumbersome process, and any student who must rely on sounding out to read many words is not reading fluently enough to concentrate on meaning.

How do children learn to become fluent readers? Which skills and mental abilities are most important and in what order? What sequence do the best practitioners and reading experts recommend? What should be taught in the skills-development strand, when should it be learned, and how does it fit with other language-arts strands?

Adams (1990, 1991; Adams & Bruck, 1995), Beck and Juel (1995), Pearson (1993), Share (1995), Stanovich (1986, 1993a), and almost all other reading experts maintain that children need explicit instruction in print concepts, phonemic awareness, decoding, word attack skills, and language structure, including phrasing, syllabic, word root, and spelling patterns—all with sufficient repetition and reinforcement so that they can learn to recognize large numbers of words automatically and decode new words efficiently. Only then will children be able to read fluently and thus be able to concentrate on meaning. It is also crucial that students develop sufficient reading proficiency at an early age so that they can use reading large amounts of text as a key method of developing fluency.

What is it about these skills that makes them so important in becoming fluent? It is important to underscore that none of these experts advocates that these component skills be the *only* strands in a reading or language arts program or that they should be taught in complete isolation from the act of reading connected text. Right from the start, children should see the purpose of reading, become instilled with a love of reading and books, think about the ideas or beauty of stories, and engage in a multitude of oral- and written-language activities. But for many children, these activities cannot replace a separate but connected age-appropriate and individually appropriate skills development component in preschool, kindergarten, and early first grade. This is what enables them to *start* reading in first grade. Subsequent skills-development strands will extend their reading and decoding skills and assist them in becoming independent learners.

To understand what beginners need to do to learn to read, it is helpful to understand why some children have difficulty learning to read. One of the biggest obstacles to word recognition, and thus to print comprehension, among less skilled readers, both in terms of automatically recognizing growing numbers of words and deciphering new words, is difficulty in decoding, that is, turning spellings into sounds (Pressley & Cariglia-Bull, 1995, pp. 30-31). Share and Stanovich (1995b) write that "We know unequivocally that less-skilled readers have difficulty turning spellings into sounds.... This relationship is so strong that it deserves to be identified as one, if not the defining feature of reading disability [citations omitted]" (p. 7). Children have difficulty learning this skill in early first grade if they have not sufficiently developed the ability to become aware of and manipulate the discrete sound segments that comprise spoken words (phonemic awareness; Adams, 1990, pp. 293-332; Juel, 1994, p. 4; Pressley & Cariglia-Bull, 1995, p. 24; Share & Stanovich, 1995b, pp. 9-10) and if they have not learned enough of the letter/sound correspondence system and word attack strategies—such as sounding out, recognizing similar letter/sound patterns, or generating alternative pronunciations for given letter patterns (phonics or decoding)—to be able to teach themselves the complete system of letter/sound patterns through extensive reading (Adams, 1990, pp. 293-332; Pressley & Cariglia-Bull, 1995, pp. 30-31; Share, 1995, p. 191).[3] Extensive reading should start in mid- to late first grade, but this ability depends on learning decoding in early first grade, which in turn depends on reaching basic levels of phonemic awareness by the end of kindergarten.

As we shall see, these two overarching abilities—phonemic awareness and decoding—are mutually dependent and reinforcing. A child cannot learn decoding without phonemic awareness, and the process of connecting letters to the pronunciations of and sounds in words is one of the best ways of learning to segment sounds.

Notes

1. Adams (1990) explains that the part of the brain concerned with meaning and context continually feeds information to the visual processing of letter patterns (and to the phonological processor) to (a) both screen out unlikely meanings of words and point to likely ones based on both accumulated knowledge of the connection of word meanings and letter patterns and (b) point to the most likely meaning of a word because of the meaning of the string of words it is in.

2. According to Share and Stanovich (1995b),

> The failure to take into account the interaction between the difficulty of materials and readers skill . . . leads to a misinterpretation of the frequent reports from teachers of children who "just plod through and don't use context." These reports usually turn out to be spurious, not because they are untrue, but because the common interpretation—that the children are plodding (recognizing words slowly) *because* they are not using context—is false. The research reviewed above leads to just the opposite conclusion: the children are not using context because they are plodding, e.g., decoding inefficiently. Given texts of equal functional difficulty, good readers would also "plod" [citations omitted]. (p. 6)

3. According to Share (1995),

> Reliable and substantial gains in reading ability have been consistently obtained in both laboratory and field settings when *both* phonemic awareness *and* symbol-sound correspondences have been trained [citations omitted]. Since training studies tend to show that neither letter-sound knowledge alone [citations omitted], nor phonemic awareness alone [citations omitted] are sufficient, we can conclude that phonemic awareness (in conjunction with letter/sound knowledge) is a causal *co-requisite* for successful reading acquisition. (p. 191)

3

Beginning-to-Read
Instruction for Preschool
and Kindergarten

Children arrive at school with varying degrees of experience with print and the sounds of language. Some children have already played with speech sounds in rhyming games and word riddles. Some enter kindergarten with a good understanding of how print works, able to recognize all the letters of the alphabet and even read some simple words. They have developed these important foundation skills by enjoying books at home—listening to books read aloud, tracking print as they follow along, discussing the different parts of stories, and sharing their reactions. Unfortunately, many children have not had these print-rich experiences and need instruction and practice in basic print concepts. These concepts are relatively easy for most students to learn. However, to make the connection between sound and print, emergent readers also need thorough alphabet recognition and a certain level of phonemic awareness. This chapter describes the early skills and concepts that lay the foundation for beginning literacy.

Listening and Responding to
Stories at School and at Home

This chapter discusses the skills strands that should be taught before first grade: the foundation skills that enable children to make the connection between sound and print. Preliminarily, it is important to reiterate that these skills should be taught in combination with regularly occurring rich oral language activities: reading good stories and informational texts to children and then discussing them; having students tell and retell stories; listening to, reciting, or singing nursery rhymes or songs, including the Alphabet Song; pretend reading, picture reading, and shared reading; playing with magnetic letters; discussing word meaning and group and individual story writing.[1]

According to David Dickinson (1994), one of the key elements distinguishing effective preschools and kindergartens from less effective ones is the nature of teacher-student talk. The more effective teachers use discussions about books and children's behavior, or even giving directions, as opportunities for encouraging children to think, predict, extend, or make personal connections. Vocabulary analysis is also important. This analytic talk can be as simple as asking children to give the reasons for a rule or tell how one story is like another (this strategy works for parents, too). These teachers use the technique judiciously; not all conversation needs to be this challenging, but enough stretching is encouraged, to make a huge difference in performance.

Dickinson found that a more didactic approach—one in which discussions of readings involved low-level recall questions, little talk before or after the story, and limited amounts of teacher and student talk during readings—was less effective. Similarly, too much teacher-student talk during readings (students continually being asked to clarify and amplify meanings) detracted from student engagement and understanding. The best approach was what Dickinson labels a performance-oriented approach, characterized by large amounts of teacher and student talk before and after the readings, such as questions connecting the story to favorite books or individual experiences. Questions during the story were limited to spontaneous analytical responses involving predictions, personal connections, and vocabulary analysis.

On the home front, Pressley and Cariglia-Bull (1995) describe how the home environment is also a major potential contributor to emergent literacy. In a literacy-nurturing environment, there are rich family conversations, ready availability of a variety of reading and writing materials and plastic letters, and parents who hold a high positive regard for literacy for themselves and their children. Such parents read to their children extensively, ask analytic questions, and value reading. Books are ubiquitous in the home, parents take children to libraries and bookstores, and television is limited. Parents can be taught successfully how to ask more analytical questions, that is, open-ended or about the attributes or functions of objects in stories (p. 22).

Naming and Recognizing Letters

A strong finding of research is that one of the best predictors of first-grade reading ability is the fast and accurate skill of naming and recognizing the shapes of letters (Adams, 1990, p. 61).[2] According to Adams's exhaustive review of the research (pp. 341-364), learning to name and accurately recognize letters is a crucial first step to reading, for the following reasons:

- A child who can recognize most letters with thorough confidence will have an easier time learning about letter sounds and word spellings than a child who also has to work at distinguishing the individual letters.
- Automatic, accurate recognition of letters as wholes frees mental energy to concentrate on recognizing patterns of letters—a key to reading.
- In general, because the names of most letters are closely associated with their sounds, children who learn to name letters also begin learning their sounds. More important, they learn to grasp what is probably the single most important understanding enabling children to learn how to read: the alphabetic principle that letters have corresponding sounds that make words when combined (Adams, 1990, pp. 63-64).

Teaching Letter Recognition

Hall and Moats (1999) recommend that the best way to learn letters is first to concentrate on learning the names of letters, then to learn to recognize their corresponding shapes, and last, to establish the concept of letter/sound correspondences. Note that this strategy is *not* to have children learn the names of letters by showing them the letters; this is backward. Children first learn the names through devices such as the Alphabet Song (usually before kindergarten) or by listening to ABC books read aloud and then learning to recognize the shape associated with that name. This latter process takes much longer and is complicated by the confusing similarities in letter shape, such as *d* and *b,* and by the fact that students have to match letter names to four written forms (uppercase manuscript, lowercase manuscript, uppercase cursive, lowercase cursive) and do so automatically and in and out of sequence. Longitudinal studies consistently have indicated that the learning of letter names comes well before the learning of their sounds. Typically, children can recite the alphabet before age 4[3] but need up to 2 years to learn the corresponding shapes.

Knowing names and shapes of letters protects children from becoming confused when they learn the sounds and ensures that students will know that the letter names are in fact names. Because phonological processing is helped by rhyme, rhythm, and pitch, songs are particularly effective ways of learning. This name/shape strategy—used in the Alphabet Song and ABC books—has proved its worth over the years and is supported and reinforced by parents who shared the same experiences. In addition, the name of the letter usually is an important clue to at least one of the sounds of the letter.

Last and of great importance, research shows that learning to identify and name letters frequently turns into interest in their sounds and in the spelling of words. Adams (1990) cites research that also shows that knowing letter names is strongly correlated with both the ability to remember the forms of written words and the tendency to treat them as ordered sequences of letters rather than holistic patterns. Conversely, the research also shows that *not* knowing letter names is coupled with extreme difficulty in learning letter sounds and word recognition. Blevins (1998) explains, "without a thorough knowledge of letters and an understanding that words are made up of sounds, children cannot learn to read."

By the end of kindergarten, students should be able to name all the uppercase and lowercase letters and match all consonant and short-vowel sounds to their corresponding letters. The goal is for them to have the rapid, accurate letter recognition they will need in first grade when they begin to focus on the more challenging task of learning to read words by sounding out and blending. Use of magnetic letters and games; the presence of classroom labels; recognition of each other's names; attention to signs; and reading, writing, and singing activities help with the task of learning to recognize letter shapes. During kindergarten, there also should be an organized effort (some combination of letter play and direct teaching that builds on phonemic awareness) to ensure that students learn a few letter/sound correspondences. According to Adams (1990),

> Learning to recognize and discriminate printed letters is just too big, too hard, and too fussy a task to be mastered incidentally, in tandem with some other hard and fussy task, or without an adult's focused attention to its progress and difficulties. . . . [W]hat a waste to correct the pronunciation of a letter sound or word if the child's confusion was really in the visual identity of the letter. (p. 363)

Writing the Letters/First Words

Writing practice is the best way to help children learn and recall letter shapes. Teachers should point out the distinctive features of each letter and help children focus on the similarities of letters they know (e.g., both *a* and *b* contain small circles.) Teachers should also point out the differences between letters that are easily confused—the direction of extenders (*b* vs. *p*), whether the letters face right or left (*b* vs. *d*), their top-bottom orientation (*m* vs. *w*), and the letters' line curve features (*u* vs. *v*). Many programs categorize letter shapes or establish motor patterns for each letter as an aid to this process. Copying, and especially tracing, are not as useful in teaching the recognition of individual letter shapes because students do not necessarily have to pay attention to either the letter's sound or its name, much less to its distinctive differences from other letters (Adams, 1990, p. 355; Clay, 1993, pp. 24-27). Kindergartners also can begin to write some easy words. As they practice writing, English language learners may need extra help understanding directional terms, such as *under, over, right, left, up,* and *down.*

The Importance of Phonemic Awareness

Phonemic awareness is the conscious understanding that spoken language is made up of individual sounds, or phonemes. *Phonological awareness* is a broader term that includes phonemic awareness as well as the ability to identify the number of words in a sentence, break a word into syllables, and to recognize and produce rhymes. Both phonemic and phonological awareness involve *spoken* language. *Phonics* involves the relationship between the sounds of spoken English and their *written* symbols. *According to the latest research, the best predictor of reading success is whether the child has developed basic phonemic awareness—the ability to consciously pick out, blend, and manipulate from* **spoken** *words the smallest sound chunks that make up those words* (Adams, 1990, p. 65; Cunningham, 1990; Juel, 1994, pp. 4, 16-17; Liberman et al., 1991, p. 12; Share & Stanovich, 1995b, pp. 9-10; Torgesen & Hecht, 1996).

Because speech is heard naturally as a continuous stream of sound, and short words and syllables are heard as one sound, preliterate individuals—whether they are children or adults—must be taught how to segment these sound chunks. For example, children and adults say and hear the word *bag* as a whole, even though it is made up of three phonemes: /b/ /a/ /g/.

Well-developed phonemic awareness is not just the ability to hear phonemes, to discriminate between two phonemes, or even to produce them. It is the ability to be conscious of these sound segments and to be able to manipulate them on demand so that all the individual sounds in a word can be connected to all the letter patterns. It took humans tens or hundreds of thousands of years to develop language. Every human language has the unique ability to combine a finite number of sounds to generate a huge number of words. In contrast, nonlanguage symbolic systems, such as traffic signs, can never have more than a few symbols.

These sound chunks are interchangeable parts, but they follow rules of combination. Humans have evolved so they can easily intuit these rules. An infant becomes a speaker of the language he or she is born into, learning how to say phonemes and combine them into words according to what is acceptable in that language. This process happens unconsciously and, for the most part, automatically. Almost every human being achieves fluency in oral language (Pinker, 1994).

Ironically, that very oral fluency is an obstacle to learning to read. Children have become so automatic and swift at hearing discrete sounds as a unified whole that they must relearn how to break up the word into its constituent sound segments. Students must become aware of how sounds generate words—the deep phonological principle behind all language—and organize that system in their long-term memory if they are to decipher an alphabetic script. In Adams's (1990) words, "To learn an alphabetic script, we must learn to attend to that which we learned not to attend to" (p. 66).

To summarize, phonemic awareness is the ability to understand consciously and analytically that words are made up of sound segments that are abstract and can be manipulated. It depends on installing that system in long-term memory and having it available to working memory when deciphering a printed word. Use of phonological knowledge is an essential prerequisite to the process of connecting the letters and patterns of letters in writing to words stored in the memory (Adams, 1990, p. 65). Beginning decoding involves reading through a word, using phonics knowledge to generate sounds for each letter or letter combination, and then blending those sounds into a recognizable word. This is not possible if students are not able to hear the sounds in words. By the end of kindergarten, all students should be able to identify at least the first and last sounds in simple CVC words. Identifying the medial sound is a more difficult task and it may take some students until early first grade, in conjunction with phonics instruction, to master it. For those who have not reached a level of phonemic awareness that enables them to profit from phonics instruction in the early grades, it must be taught, or 90% of these children will fail to learn to read in first grade and will never recover (Blachman, 1991).[4] Isabelle and Alvin Liberman, respected researchers in this field, estimated that 30% of students they sampled did not understand the internal phonemic structure of words even at the end of a full year of school. In their opinion, almost every poor reader has a very weak understanding of this phonological structure (Liberman et al., 1991; see also Adams, 1990, p. 293 et seq.; Juel, 1994, pp. 1-24; Lundberg, 1991).

Some people have argued that because children all learn to speak effortlessly without being taught, they should learn to read just as easily—the naturalist fallacy. The English written language is based on an amazing human invention, the alphabetic principle, which stems from the insight that words have an internal structure and can be broken into sound chunks that then can be represented by letters and combinations of letters to constitute written words. Many sophisticated cultures never developed a writing system based on this alphabetic system. To expect children to discover on their own what a few unsung geniuses figured out very recently in our species' history is hopelessly romantic. The vast findings of the scientific and research communities refute the proposition that most children can accomplish this task unaided (Share & Stanovich, 1995b, pp. 31-32). In fact, these findings strongly indicate just the opposite: Most children need help in developing phonemic awareness before they can map letters and letter combinations to spoken words and map language onto the printed page (Pressley & Rankin, 1994, p. 161). In contrast, children are genetically predisposed to learn how to speak and understand language without much adult assistance (Pinker, 1994).

Numerous research studies of nonliterate peoples, nonreaders, and children before they learn to read—all of whom have great difficulty in segmenting spoken words into phonemes—have confirmed these findings. These findings also have been confirmed in studies of children born with profound hearing deficiencies, who have never heard language. Many of these children will read 2 to 3 years below grade level. The ones who do reach high levels of reading proficiency have invariably figured out the phonological principle by alternative methods, such as oral training, lipreading, or seeing spelling patterns (Liberman et al., 1991, pp. 21-22). Other risk factors have been identified for phonemic awareness deficiencies. These include speech impairments, phonological processing problems, learning English as a second language, and coming from a literacy-deprived environment.

Teaching Phonemic Awareness

There are three important instructional issues. First, *throughout kindergarten, all students should spend at least 15 minutes a day developing their phonemic awareness* by playing with the sounds of language. There are many ways to incorporate fun activities as a warm-up to daily reading instruction—making up rhymes, singing songs, chanting along with puppets, and playing circle games (Blevins, 1998; Honig et al., 2000). The second crucial issue is *assessment at midyear* to determine who is and isn't reaching the basic level of phonemic awareness—the ability to identify the first sound in spoken words. Researchers estimate that 1 out of 6 children have an extremely difficult time acquiring this basic level of phonemic awareness and cannot isolate the first sound in words such as *cap* and *get*. The third issue is the critical need for *early intervention*. By providing 12 to 14 additional hours of intensive phonemic awareness training in mid to late kindergarten, the vast majority of these at-risk students will be able to reach the level of phonemic awareness necessary for phonics instruction (Torgesen, 1997).

Phonological awareness generally follows a developmental sequence. Awareness of words, rhymes, and syllables typically occurs in the preschool and kindergarten years. Awareness of phonemes occurs later, generally beginning in kindergarten and further developed in first grade. Phonemic awareness should be the focus of instruction rather than earlier skills, such as rhyme recognition. The following five-stage developmental sequence shows the progression of tasks that lead to the recognition of the first and last sounds and the blending and segmenting of CVC words:

1. *Word Segmentation:* the ability to identify the number of words in a sentence. Prompt: "How many words are there in the sentence, *'I like bananas?'"*

2. *Rhyme Recognition and Production:* the ability to hear and produce rhymes. Prompts: "Does *pie* rhyme with *sky?*" "What rhymes with *pie?*" Note that some kindergartners who can identify the initial and final sound in a CVC word may not be able to rhyme. This is not a cause for concern.

3. *Syllable Blending, Segmentation, and Deletion:* the ability to blend syllables to pronounce a word, break a word into syllables, and to say a word without one of its syllables. Prompts: "Listen to the two word parts—*base . . . ball.* Now say the whole word." "Say the two word parts in *baseball.*" "Say *baseball* without *ball.*" Note that blending is usually easier than segmenting, which is easier than deletion.

4. *Onset and Rime Blending:* the ability to blend the *onset* of a syllable (initial consonant, consonant blend, or consonant digraph) with the *rime* (vowel and everything that follows it). Prompts: "What word am I trying to say: /ch/ . . . *op?*

5. *Phoneme Matching and Isolation:* the ability to recognize the same sound in different words and to identify the sounds in a given word. Students typically master this skill with initial phonemes in midkindergarten. Prompt: "What is the first sound you hear in *cap?*" The more difficult task of matching and isolating final and medial phonemes generally doesn't occur until late kindergarten and early first grade. Prompt: "What is the last/middle sound you hear in *cap?*"

Next in the developmental sequence are *phoneme blending* and *phoneme segmentation.* These are the most difficult phonemic awareness skills in kindergarten and the most important for decoding. Phoneme blending is the ability to blend together individual sounds to pronounce an entire word. Prompt: "Can you guess the word I am trying to say: /k/ /a/ /p/?" Phoneme segmentation is the ability to count the number of sounds in a word and to identify those sounds in sequence. Prompts: "How many sounds do you hear in *cap?*" "What sounds do you hear in *cap?*" Ideally, instruction in phoneme blending and segmentation should begin in the first few months of kindergarten so that by early first grade, students can fully segment a CVC or CCVC word to decode it.

Later, as students have more practice connecting print to sound, they develop the more advanced skills of deleting and substituting phonemes and segmenting more complex language structures. These advanced skills should not be included in the kindergarten curriculum.

Phonemic Awareness Activities

Every kindergarten program should aim at ensuring that students enter first grade with basic phonemic awareness. Research clearly indicates that phonemic awareness can be developed through instruction and that instruction significantly accelerates children's subsequent reading and writing achievement (Ball & Blachman, 1991; Foorman, Francis, Shaywitz, Shaywitz, & Fletcher, 1997; Torgesen, 1997). Obviously, students come to kindergarten with different levels of these skills; instruction should be flexible enough to respond to differing needs. Most phonemic instructional activities start with extensive games and word play and then move on to more directed activities, such as matching and isolating, blending, segmenting, and manipulating oral sounds and connecting sounds with letters. These activities can still be gamelike and thus should fit in well with other kindergarten activities.

A sophisticated range of phonemic awareness activities with spoken language has been developed during the past few years. These programs, now available for use in classrooms, have produced significant advances in phonemic awareness.[5] They include rhyming activities; identifying the beginning, middle, or ending sounds; or identifying words spoken in a broken fashion (/p/, /i/, /g/); identifying word families, such as *s-ing, r-ing, th-ing;* counting or matching the sounds of words with counters and letters (Blachman, 1991, pp. 7-19; Griffith & Olson, 1992; Yopp, 1992); and training students to be aware of how their tongues and lips make sound (Lindamood, Bell, & Lindamood, 1992). Phonemic training can give children practice "feeling" where sounds are made and can teach them how to produce different sounds by changing the position of the tongue and lips, controlling air flow, and vibrating the vocal cords. Such explicit instruction in manipulating and articulating the sounds of spoken language is of particular benefit to English language learners.

Used in the classroom, phonemic awareness programs can have a tremendous impact on a child's learning. As an example, Blachman and Ball initiated a very successful phonological awareness training in inner-city kindergartens in upstate New York. Groups of four to five children were taught for 4 days a week for 11 weeks, for 15 to 20 minutes a day—the equivalent of approximately 11 to 15 hours of training. Kindergarten teachers and aides received 14 hours of inservice training (Blachman, 1991).

The lesson consisted of three parts. First, the children engaged in an activity called *say-it-and-move-it,* in which they represented each sound in a one-, two-, or three-phoneme word with a blank tile. Later, they used tiles with letters they had already learned to recognize. Research has shown that connecting letters and sounds is reciprocally related and enhances the teaching of both (Blachman, 1991, p. 11).

The second activity comprised a variety of segmentation-related activities, such as odd-picture-out. The third activity was learning letters and their sounds. Large increases in phoneme segmentation ability, letter knowledge, and reading and spelling occurred (Blachman, 1991, pp. 14-15). *Imagine the implications: Most children who will fail at beginning-reading tasks are only 14 hours away from removing a major barrier to succeeding in first grade, if the right intervention is provided early enough.* In fact, as little as 15 to 20 minutes a day of small-group intervention 3 to 4 days a week for about 10 weeks can prevent reading difficulties in most students (Adams, Foorman, Lundberg, & Beeler, 1998).

The Lindamood-Bell Learning Process[6] also produces effective phonemic training, but the programs require more time with a broader representation of kindergartners. The strategies include some analytic word activities, such as learning how sounds are made with the mouth and tongue; using chips to become conscious of words, sounds, similarities, and differences; then progressing to using letters; and last, performing multisyllabic segment comparison tasks. More extensive phonemic awareness training may be necessary for extremely phonologically challenged children. Three effective intervention programs are *Auditory Discrimination in Depth* (Lindamood & Lindamood, 1984), *Phonological Awareness Training for Reading* (Torgesen & Bryant, 1994), and *Phonemic Awareness in Young Children: A Classroom Curriculum* (Adams et al., 1998).

Whichever method is used, it is essential to ensure that every kindergarten child has the opportunity to receive the phonemic support he or she needs. This means a midkindergarten assessment of all youngsters on phonemic awareness scales that shows whether students know the segmental nature of speech. There are a number of resources for assessing phonological awareness, including *Lindamood Auditory Conceptualization Test,; Test of Auditory Analysis Skills,* and *Test of Phonological*

Awareness. The *Phonological Awareness Screening Test* in *CORE Assessing Reading: Multiple Measures* (CORE, 2000) is a screening tool that can be administered to all kindergarten children midyear, to first graders in the fall, and to second graders who are not yet reading. The test contains six subtests that assess students' ability to (a) detect rhymes, (b) count syllables, (c) match initial sounds, (d) count phonemes, (e) compare word lengths, and (f) represent phonemes with letters. By the middle of kindergarten, normally progressing students should be able to match pictures of objects with rhyming names (clock and sock), tally the number of syllables in a picture's name (alligator: 4), and match pictures whose names begin with the same initial sound (heart and hand). By the end of kindergarten or early first grade, students should be able to tally the number of phonemes in a picture's name (soap: 3; broom: 4) and to choose the picture that represents the word with more sounds (bread vs. bed).[7]

Children also need to be assessed periodically to determine progress with tasks such as blending; identifying beginning, middle, and ending sounds in spoken words; and letter-to-sound mapping tasks. By late kindergarten to early first grade, all students should be able to identify words that end with the same sound and produce CVC words by blending together the phonemes. Those who cannot will require more intensive phonemic-awareness instruction.

Print Concepts

Before they enter first grade, most middle-class youngsters have developed basic print awareness, or what Marie Clay (1991) calls "concepts about print," through more than 1,000 hours of parental attention that includes being read to and other print activities, such as playing with magnetic letters, puzzles, games, and so on. These concepts include the purpose of reading, the structure of written text, how stories work, what a word is, how words are composed of letters, what white spaces signify, and directionality—that is, how print is organized, which necessitates the ability to scan left to right and then sweep diagonally left and one line down (Clay, 1991, pp. 141-154).

In contrast, many lower socioeconomic children have been read to for fewer than 50 hours and are way behind their middle-class peers in acquiring basic print awareness. These students must be given these experiences in Head Start programs, preschool programs, and kindergarten through a combination of language activities in which these concepts can be pointed out or through games that allow manipulation of letters, words, and sentences. Reading English print involves several discrete movements: tracking the letters within a word from left to right, tracking words on a line from left to right, tracking text from the top to the bottom of a page, sweeping to the next line, and tracking sentences across pages. These print concepts may be difficult for students who have learned to read in languages that are nonalphabetic (e.g., Chinese, Japanese, Urdu), use different writing systems (e.g., Arabic, Korean, Russian, Vietnamese) or different directional conventions (e.g., Arabic, Chinese, Urdu). Marie Clay (1991) has developed a widely used Concepts in Print assessment and has suggested a wealth of print awareness activities for children (pp. 145-154).

Mastering a Few Sight Words

Only 100 words account for approximately 50% of all the words in English print (Fry, Fountoukidis, & Polk, 1995). By the end of kindergarten, students should be able to recognize 25 to 50 of these *high-frequency* words instantly, on sight. This provides them with the basic tools they need to begin to practice reading coherent, engaging text that contains words with previously taught letter/sound correspondences as well as previously introduced high-frequency and story words.

Systematic instruction in high-frequency words should begin as soon as students understand the concept of a word and can recognize and name the letters of the alphabet. Daily practice can include finding words on a word wall, solving riddles, chanting the spellings, and writing high-frequency words in sentences the teacher dictates. Initially, the number of words introduced at one time should be limited to as few as 1 or 2 per week, gradually increasing to about 3 to 7 words per week in first grade.

Words that follow regular, predictable spelling patterns (e.g., *and, that, with, be, not*) can be taught as whole words before students have learned all of the individual letter/sound correspondences. When introducing irregular words (e.g., *of, to, you, was, are, have*), it is important that teachers help students focus on all the letter patterns and point out the specific irregularities. This is because even when decoding an irregular word, readers rely on sound/symbol information. For the first few times teachers introduce irregular words, Carnine, Silbert, and Kameenui (1997) recommend they model the correct pronunciation of a word and then contrast it with the way the word would sound if each letter or letter pattern had its most common sound (e.g. the correct pronunciation of *was* (/w/ /u/ /z/) vs. /w/ /a/ /s/).

A spell-out strategy helps students learn irregular words *prior to encountering them in text* by focusing their attention on all of the letter patterns. With this method, students see and hear the word, say the word, spell it letter by letter, and repeat the word. Sounding out with contextual analysis is the recommended strategy for figuring out unfamiliar words *as they are encountered in text*. With this method, students use phonics and structural cues to arrive at an approximate pronunciation and then use context to confirm or correct the pronunciation. For example, when children first come across the irregular word *put*, they may mispronounce it as *putt*. By using the context of the sentence, *"I put the hat in the box,"* they will arrive at the correct word.

Syntactic Awareness

Last, teaching preschool and kindergarten students about sentences, phrases, and the order of words by bringing these concepts to their attention in reading activities or through manipulative games has been shown to improve reading ability (Clay, 1991, pp. 293-295). As Adams (1990) writes, "With respect to young readers, development of syntactic competence may be far more important than is generally recognized in reading instruction."

Summary

Any successful reading program must start with a skills strand in preschool or Head Start and continue to build on it with a skills strand in kindergarten. It must explicitly include activities that teach the names and shapes of letters and, as much as possible, their most common sounds, because some have more than one. It must include beginning phonemic awareness and print and syntactic awareness, in addition to the strands that stress oral language; listening to, discussing, and retelling stories; and writing group stories.

Activities to develop oral language and print awareness have become widespread. Most preschools and kindergartens incorporate shared reading of stories with big books that enable a class of children to follow along. Research-based programs use a strategy of having children retell stories to develop active engagement with books. Many teachers read and discuss good children's literature and write down dictated stories from the children or have children learn to write letters and try to write stories.

What is also needed is a *systematic* strategy for developing an increasing knowledge of the other important prerequisites for reading—knowing the names of letters, their shapes, and the more simple sounds associated with some of them, understanding the internal phonological structure of spoken words,[8] recognition of high-frequency words, and a basic understanding of syntax.

Notes

1. For a good summary of these ideas, see Hoorn, Nourot, and Scales (1993). According to these authors, children develop precursors to reading during ages 3 to 5 through play and investigations. These include

- Learning to use symbols to represent experiences (a block being used as a telephone)
- Taking the perspective of others
- Using increasingly efficient mental strategies to remember information and solve problems
- Predicting
- Developing story plays for self and their peers to "act out" and thus learning story grammars, such as plot, character development, and so on (pp. 20-25, 133-147, 193-216, 220-225)

2. Adams elaborates:

The orthographic processor cannot begin to learn spellings until it has learned to recognize the letters from which they must be built. The phonological processor cannot usefully learn letter sounds until the orthographic processor has learned to discriminate the individual letters with which they must be linked. (p. 362)

3. English-speaking children in California could name on average 71% of uppercase letters by age 5. Spanish-speaking children could identify on average only 4%. See Adams (1990, p. 358, ft. 69). In contrast, most children learn to recite the letter names, as in the Alphabet Song, before age 4 or even age 3. For longitudinal studies on learning names well before shapes, see Adams (1990, p. 360, ft. 77).

4. Blachman (1991) writes that

One of the fundamental tasks facing the beginning reader is to develop the realization that speech can be segmented and that these segmented units can be represented by printed forms. . . . As we now know from

extensive research conducted during the last fifteen years, developing
an awareness of the phonological segments in words is an important prerequisite to understanding how an alphabetic transcription represents
speech. That transcription will make sense to beginning readers only if
they understand that the transcription has the same number and sequence of units as the spoken word [citation omitted]. (pp. 5-7)

5. See study cited in Torgesen and Barker (1995) in which Wagner, Torgesen,
and Rashotte looked at 13 phonological awareness training studies in 1993 and
found large average effect size of about $1\frac{1}{4}$ standard deviations (moving a child
from the 50th percentile to above the 70th) in phonemic awareness.

6. Lindamood-Bell Learning Process, 416 Higuera St., San Luis Obispo, California 93401, Tel: (805) 541-3836.

7. Even for adults, segmenting words into their constituent sounds is a difficult task. We have become so adept at translating the sounds of English into their
alphabetic representation that we are not aware of the individual sound segments
in words like *uncle* or *frog*. For this reason, many educators have to teach themselves how to segment and manipulate phonemes. Tasks such as counting the number of phonemes in *ox* or saying *enough* backwards can be a challenge.

8. Some of the newest reading series offer a balanced approach between literature-based instruction and systematic, explicit skills development. These materials offer letter recognition, phonemic awareness, concepts of print, phonics
instruction, blending practice, word work, syntactic understanding, and the other
skills described in this section.

4

Beginning-to-Read Instruction for Early First Grade

Several issues are central to early first-grade reading instruction, as follows:

1. Students need to be taught enough about the phonemic, phonic, syntactic, and word structure systems and provided with sufficient word attack and other self-teaching strategies to enable them to automatically recognize a critical mass of common words and know how to decode simple new words.

2. Once students attain this much control of the reading process, they can then begin to read larger and larger amounts of narrative and informational text. Reading more text of increasing complexity depends on two elements—becoming automatic with more words and increasing decoding skills. The reason automaticity is so important is that if readers take too much time and mental effort decoding individual words, they can't attend to the meaning of the passage. The rule of thumb is that students should recognize 18 or 19 out of 20 words automatically—that is, 95% of the words, or reading comprehension suffers. Because it takes between 4 and 15 successful attempts at an individual word before that

word becomes automatically recognized (if decoded the first few times by looking through all of the letter patterns, generating all of the corresponding sounds, and blending the sounds into a word), students need to read enough to become automatic with growing numbers of words. This growing automaticity then increases the kinds of books they can read and still stay within the accepted range of manageable text.

3. If instruction in the more complex decoding skills is also provided, even more material will be available to students. One of the main barriers to extensive reading is that in English, text is replete with many words important to the meaning of the passage but that occur infrequently (with little chance for the word to become automatic). Without a system for decoding these words independently, students are effectively cut off from much potentially engaging, instructionally important, but increasingly complex, material.

4. Developing a growing pool of automatically recognized words and increasingly sophisticated decoding skills will enable students to read extensively and learn the rest of the phonics, syntax, and word structure systems as they tackle progressively more difficult books and stories. This independent and assigned reading should be monitored by teachers who provide reinforcement, guidance, continual assessment, and direct teaching to fill in the gaps.

In addition to accelerating and broadening the processes of becoming fluent readers, extensive reading also will help students develop a love of literature, learn about the world through fiction and nonfiction, and enrich their lives. Simultaneously, instruction should include strands of reading to children, reading strategically, discussing material, writing, mechanics, and spelling.

If students are to reach this level—able to read and learn from trade books and basal texts without struggling with most words—then, as argued earlier, most of them will first need to be directly taught enough phonemic awareness, basic phonics, and word attack skills in an organized, sequential, active-learning program. A key component of this strategy is guiding the student to think about the phonemic system (how sounds make up words), the alphabetic connections (which letter patterns make which sounds and words), the syntactic structures (do the words sound right in context?), and meaning (does the word make sense?) while students read high-quality stories and materials designed specifically to (or are appropriate to) reinforce the skills being taught. Students also need ample opportunities to practice translating sounds and words into print through writing, spelling, and word play activities.

The following sections discuss the essential details, strategy, and timing of each of the key skills that must be taught.

Decoding and Comprehension

The ability to decode, or sound out words, is the key to comprehension in first grade. This is because most of the words in beginning texts are familiar and part of students' oral vocabulary, so the words only need to be decoded to be understood. Automatic and rapid word recognition depends on this initial, accurate decoding, which in turn depends on phonics and word attack skills, which in turn depend on the foundation skills of print concepts, alphabet recognition, and phonemic awareness.

Connie Juel (1994) has written one of the clearest explanations of what it takes to teach low-socioeconomic children to read and why in *Learning to Read and Write in One Elementary School*. She is another leading researcher who maintains that one of the clearest findings of research is that first-grade reading comprehension is almost exclusively determined by word recognition (p. 12). Lyon (1994) confirms these findings; the ability to read and comprehend depends on rapid and automatic recognition and decoding of single words, and slow and inaccurate decoding are the best predictors of difficulties in reading comprehension (research cited, p. 11). Juel (1994) found that the ability to recognize single words in print accounted for 71% of ending first-grade reading comprehension among a group of poor children she studied (p. 17). The other major factor—listening comprehension, or the ability to understand spoken words—only contributed 6%. Listening comprehension becomes much more important in second grade and beyond as material becomes more difficult and the ability to read words develops (Juel, 1994, p. 17).

The Connecticut Longitudinal Study (Foorman et al., 1997) shows that first-grade decoding ability continues to be a major factor in text comprehension as students progress through the grades. How well a student learned to decode in first grade correlates about 40% with comprehension in fourth grade and about 27% in ninth grade. Learning to decode words in first grade provides students with the basic tools they need to practice reading, and this practice enables them to increase the number of words they recognize automatically.

Recognizing Single Words

Automaticity—rapid, effortless, and unconscious word recognition—is a critical goal of all reading instruction. There are two paths to automaticity: the ability to decode and lexical knowledge. Some educators use *decoding* and *automaticity* as synonymous terms. In this book, I use *decoding* to refer to the conscious and deliberate process of sounding out word parts (single letters, letter strings, phonograms, and syllables) to come up with a plausible pronunciation of a word that is not immediately recognized. Lexical knowledge is the memorized knowledge of the internal letter structure of words. Students who rely solely on lexical knowledge without knowing the systematic ways that print maps to sound have no means to decipher new and different words. In first grade, lexical knowledge determines only about one fourth of the ability to recognize words, whereas ciphering or decoding determines about two thirds. By second grade, the contribution of ciphering goes down to one fourth and the automatic—unmediated by tracking letter to sound—lexical recognition jumps to more than one half of all words, as students become familiar with more and more words (Juel, 1994, p. 17). However, it is crucial that beginning readers establish the pathways for automatic retrieval of these rapidly recognized words through the tool of decoding which makes the sound/symbol connection in the mind and allows for accessible storage and quick retrieval. As will be discussed later in this chapter, storing words in long-term memory without letter/sound patterns results in appreciably slower recognition.

Learning to Decode

Decoding is the process of converting a printed word into its spoken form. It involves looking at a word and connecting the letter patterns with sounds and blending those sounds together to form a spoken word. Decoding is essential because it is the only way to get enough information about a word—its sounds and unique letter patterns connected to its meaning—to subsequently develop automatic recognition of that word. Learning to decode (knowing letter/sound patterns and word attack skills) in turn depends primarily on phonemic awareness (contributing about one half to decoding ability in both first and second grades) and alphabetic knowledge and secondarily on exposure to print (the number of words that have been read correctly). Exposure to print contributes about one third in first grade and one fourth in second grade to decoding ability (Juel, 1994).[1] Syntactic and context knowledge also help with decoding, but make much smaller contributions. Phonemic awareness is a prerequisite or corequisite for decoding skills. Attempting to teach phonics without attending to phonemic awareness is destined to fail (Juel, 1994, pp. 16-24). Lyon (1994) adds that "the ability to decode single words accurately and fluently is dependent upon the ability to segment words and syllables into abstract constituent sound units (phonemes). Deficits in phonological awareness reflect the core deficit in dyslexia [research cited]" (p. 11).

Juel (1994) reached her conclusions by following a cohort of low-income children from first to fourth grade. She determined which students were average or above in reading comprehension in the fourth grade and which were in the bottom quartile and then went back to the assessments made in early and late first grade, early and late second grade, and so on, to see which factors made the difference.

On a 42-item phonemic awareness scale, the students who ended up in the bottom quartile at the end of fourth grade scored about 4 at the beginning of first grade and only improved to 19 at the end of first grade. Members of the average-to-top group of readers started first grade at 21 (above where the low group finished) and went all the way to 38 (just about maximum on the phonemic awareness scale) by the end of first grade, a level not reached by the low group until the end of third grade. Thus, during the crucial period of early first grade when the average and good readers had the ability and desire to learn phonics, they did, and so learned to read. In contrast, the low group (remember, all these children came from similar backgrounds) learned very little about decoding—except bad habits and frustration. Because they were not taught phonemic awareness, they could not comprehend being asked to "say the first sound in *apple*," they could not learn to sound out a word, and they could not learn new letter/sound correspondences from printed words.

As a result, on a ciphering test (which uses pseudowords such as *buf* and *dit* so memorized words make no difference), the average-to-good readers scored 25. The first 20 words on this test were simple CVC words; the next 20 were more complex, such as *cleef,* and the last 10 were multisyllabic. The low group scored only 8 despite a year's instruction in phonics and reading (about 40% of the low group could not read a single word on the list—none of these children had any phonemic awareness at the beginning of first grade). The good-reader group made substantial progress in second grade and hit very high levels on this phonics test by the end of third grade—scoring in the mid to high 40s—and then grew slightly after that. The poor readers progressed slowly from a lower base, hit 28 at the end of third grade, and stayed there.[2]

There are four main reasons why students struggle when learning to decode. First, they may not have enough phonemic awareness to segment or blend sounds in words—skills that are necessary to learn phonics. Second, they may not have learned enough about the ways that different consonant and vowel sounds are represented by the letters of the alphabet. Third, they may have learned the system of letter/sound correspondences but may have difficulty applying that knowledge in sounding out new words. Fourth, they may not have had enough practice reading words that contain the basic patterns to become automatic with a large number of words.

Not remedying these sources of decoding difficulty early in the first grade dooms children to failure. Only one out of eight children who are not reading at grade level by the end of first grade will ever read on grade level (Juel, 1994, p. 24).[3] Reading becomes frustrating and embarrassing, with the result that these bottom quartile children begin to actively dislike reading and end up reading much less than their counterparts. Juel found that by fourth grade, the average-to-top group read almost four times as much at home and twice as much in school. By fourth grade, only one out of five students in the poor reading group said unequivocally that they liked to read, in contrast to 9 out of 10 of the good-reader group. Forty percent of the poor readers would rather clean their room than read compared to only 5% of the average- and good-reader groups. Or as one of the poor readers said, "I'd rather clean the mold around the bathtub than read" (Juel, 1994, p. 120).

Since extensive reading is the only way to ensure that students make adequate progress in vocabulary growth, and since it takes about two years to perfect basic reading fluency, every failure in acquiring skills thwarts the amount of reading necessary for growth. To learn the 3,000 to 4,000 words a year required to maintain grade-level reading, by the fifth grade students should be reading more than 1.1 million words a year in outside, independent reading. Yet according to a study of fifth-grade readers ranked by their amount of independent reading, only one quarter of the students read that number of words per year and those in the bottom quartile read between one-tenth and one-fortieth of the required number of words (Anderson, Wilson, & Fielding, 1988).

By reading so little, children cut themselves off from the best activity to improve their reading and thinking capacity in the primary years (Cunningham & Stanovich, 1993, p. 201; Stanovich, 1993a). Low-income or second language children depend more heavily on school experiences to expand their vocabulary and conceptual knowledge than higher-socioeconomic-status children. For them and most other children, extensive reading is the major factor in producing further growth in reading and listening comprehension, concept and vocabulary growth, and fluency, which in turn are all critical to further reading. Consequently, being able to read early becomes crucial in becoming more literate.

Reading and Comprehension

Juel's (1994) study of low-income good and poor readers demonstrates how important widespread reading is in improving the conceptual capacity of low-income students. In that study, listening comprehension was extremely low for both groups in the beginning of first grade; both good and poor readers scored about 1.5 on a 6-point scale. By the end of second grade, the low group reached 2.5 on this listening test and did not improve after that. The average to top group improved to 3.2 at the end of second grade, to 4.9 at the end of third grade, and 5.2 at the end of fourth grade (p. 22).

Consequently, disadvantaged children can substantially improve their knowledge about the world, the depth of their conceptual understanding, and their vocabulary—all of which are key determinants of further advances in reading—by extensive in-school and at-home reading. In fourth grade, growth in listening comprehension slowed for the top group as the conceptual load of books in subjects such as science and history increased. At this stage, further growth begins to depend more on instruction in strategic reading (knowing when and how to use key comprehension strategies); understanding narrative and expository text organization; morphemic analysis and syllabication; effective book discussions; and independent, wide reading, all of which are discussed in later chapters.

Thus, the ability to read early becomes crucial to later reading success, and those who miss out in the early first grade almost never recover. Stanovich (1986) called this phenomenon the "Matthew effect"—the rich get richer and the poor get poorer. Juel (1994) explains this phenomenon as follows:

A lack of phonemic awareness severely limits children's growth in cipher knowledge, which in turn limits their ability to recognize words and to spell, which ultimately acts to constrain growth in listening comprehension and ideas that will in turn limit reading comprehension and writing. (p. 121)

In summary, without organized intervention during this critical early stage, the educational careers of these slow-to-start readers have already been determined. However, experts estimate that significant numbers of this bottom quartile can get on track by the end of first grade, either with effective initial teaching or rapid supplemental intervention when problems become apparent. Juel (1994), for example, enables three out of four students with extremely low levels of phonemic awareness in early first grade to achieve grade level in comprehension by the end of first grade. She reaches additional students during second grade through a tutoring program teaching phonemic awareness and deciphering mainly through reading, writing, and word activities aimed at learning these skills.

Practice Makes Perfect: The Sequence of Becoming an Automatic Reader

Experience and research of the past two decades, including studies such as Juel's, have led educators Linnea Ehri (1994, pp. 325-343, 1995) and David Share and Keith Stanovich (1995b, pp. 13-27; see also Share, 1995) to delineate the phases by which a student becomes an automatic reader. Share and Stanovich (1995b) call their model the "self-teaching model" because the act of repetitive decoding of a particular word and connecting spelling to sounds (which they call "phonological recoding") helps establish the spelling patterns of that word in memory. Each time the letters in the word are read successfully, the sound is heard mentally, the pathways for access get stronger, and that word becomes a little easier to recognize the next time it is encountered, until reading it becomes automatic. In the early stages of reading, it takes about four or five times of successfully decoding a word for it to become fully automatic. Encountering the word in the context of reading, as opposed to in isolation, reduces the number of successful attempts necessary. (For some special education students, the number of necessary readings may reach 50 or 100.) The most effective way for students to become fluent with a specific word is for them to consciously process both the letter patterns and sounds of the word the first few times it is read (Ehri, 1994; Share, 1995; Share & Stanovich, 1995b). For beginning readers, a combination of repeated reading of familiar material and tackling new material builds a critical mass of automatically recognized words, which in turn multiplies the number of books a student can read.

At the same time students are becoming automatic with a growing number of words, they are strengthening their ability to decode new words by establishing different patterns of spelling/sound correspondences. Last, by repeated successful attempts at recognizing individual words, not only do those words become automatic, but the letter and sound pattern of each word also gets added to the generalized knowledge about the spelling sound system and is available to help decode other words. Full alphabetic decoding enables students to become automatic with a growing number of words. Without this critical tool, they must resort to memorization or slower and less accurate contextual strategies to recognize words (Stanovich, 1986).

Phases in Reading Development

Ehri (1994, 1995) identifies four phases in developing automatic recognition of words on sight: (a) prealphabetic, (b) partial alphabetic, (c) full alphabetic, and (d) consolidated alphabetic. These phases are not hard and fast, and as students acquire more knowledge about how written language works and become automatic with a growing number of words, they use a mix of strategies. To become proficient readers, however, students must be able to generate all the sounds in spoken words, blend the discrete sounds for letter patterns, and must understand the underlying structures that help them process larger units of print in the later phases of reading development. It is not until students enter the fully alphabetic stage that they have enough information stored for subsequent rapid retrieval. Context clues, or even being told a word when stumped, also help supplement the initial stages of learning to recognize a word and can speed up the process of retrieving a partially decoded word (Share & Stanovich, 1995b; Tunmer & Chapman, 1995), but as explained, these methods are too inefficient and too slow to be relied on as a major strategy for the self-teaching model.[4]

Prealphabetic Phase

The first phase, which is actually prereading, occurs early in kindergarten and is extremely short-lived. In this stage, children recognize words by distinctive visual cues in or around the word; for example, the McDonald's arch, the patterns of letters in their name, or the two *z's* in *pizza*. This strategy does not take them too far because most words' shapes are not that distinctive, there is no system for linking spelling to pronunciation, and, most important, students have no method for reading new words. Too much reliance on shape and visual features can actually slow down the learning-to-read process (Share & Stanovich, 1995b, p. 20).

Partial Alphabetic Phase

The second phase, partial alphabetic, occurs after students acquire some early letter and sound knowledge, which for most children should be under way by the kindergarten years. Students look for a few salient letter/sound cues to read words. The cues are partial, involving only the first or last letter in a word. This stage starts the path to rapid access to words through the alphabetic principal as students look for some letter/ sound correspondence. Obviously, children need a basic level of phonemic awareness, knowledge of some specific letter shapes and names, and a smattering of specific letter/sound correspondences (Share & Stanovich, 1995b, p. 21). This partial decoding stage is helpful in starting to lay down in students' minds letter/sound correspondences in advance of learning functional decoding skills. However, this strategy is not very effective in identifying words because many words in English are so similar (e.g., *house* and *horse*) and cannot be identified by partial decoding strategies.

Overlapping this partial alphabetic phase is the growing ability of beginning readers to recognize words by memorizing their spelling (logographical or lexical learning by the use of spelling patterns alone, as opposed to alphabetic learning) but without being able to sound out the word. This is the way many nonalphabetic languages, such as Chinese, are learned. Many kindergartners and first graders have memorized a considerable number of words, especially high-frequency words, without knowing decoding skills. But memorizing words as a strategy to learn to read has fatal flaws in English.

First, memorizing increasing numbers of words becomes a difficult burden for most children. According to Stanford University Education Professor Robert Calfee (Calfee & Patrick, 1995, pp. 79-80), English calls for a deeper understanding of the alphabetic principle than other alphabetic languages because there are so many basic three-letter CVC groups in English—more than 10,000 variations and far too many to learn by one-by-one memorizing. In Connie Juel's (1994) study, first-grade students (there were two groups) encountered 1,000 to 1,500 different words in their first-grade basal readers. In contrast, Chinese children who learn primarily logographically—by the visual form of the word—learn only 3,500 characters in 6 years of school, and Chinese words and characters are much more visually distinctive (Juel, 1994, p. 11).

Second, memorizing words does not help children learn how to decipher the large number of new but infrequently encountered words that occur in English text. Thus, it is not a powerful enough technique to help them read increasing amounts of new material and capitalize on effective self-teaching strategies. These findings explain why, as previously discussed, lack of decoding ability is the primary reason students fail to progress in reading proficiency. This logographic as opposed to alphabetic strategy was the basis for the old "look-say method" that Chall (1983, 1989, 1992, 1995) found to be so much less effective than code-based strategies. Those students who did learn to read under look-say methods intuited the sound/symbol relationship. Many students never made the connection.[5]

Full Alphabetic Phase

In the next phase, students learn the basic letter/sound correspondences and can use them to sound out simple words. As more correspondences are learned, students are able to accurately decode a growing number of words by connecting all the letter patterns with sounds, generating the sounds, and then blending them together into a recognizable word. This process of full decoding is the key to automaticity. This alphabetic ability considerably extends the potential words that can be decoded and learned, increases the number of books that can be read, and allows more attention to meaning, as less time must be spent deciphering those words.

However, simple phonics, by itself, is not enough to achieve complete and automatic recognition for many irregular words that cannot be deciphered solely by attempting to match sounds to letters. For example, blending works for *sip* or even *slip,* but not for *slight.* Students must also begin to recognize the larger chunks of letter patterns (e.g., recurring phonograms and word endings) and some whole-word spelling patterns, translating those patterns into their pronunciations, and creating a representation of that pattern and word in memory—capabilities that also develop during this phase. More important, letter/pattern sound knowledge helps in decoding and remembering irregular words (Share & Stanovich, 1995b, p. 23). According to Share and Stanovich,

> Most irregular words, when encountered in natural text, have sufficient letter-sound regularity (primarily consonantal) to permit selection of the correct target among a set of candidate pronunciations. . . . [Thus], an approximate or partial decoding may be adequate for learning irregular words encountered in the course of everyday reading. (p. 23; see also Share, 1995, p. 166)

This alphabetic phase, usually beginning in early first grade, is when true reading can start. Students using this alphabetic strategy need to have decoding skills (mapping each letter and letter pattern to a sound), blending and word attack skills, and a growing number of word-family spelling/sound patterns. Students also need to know how to apply these skills in reading for meaning and read enough text to expand their alphabetic knowledge. If students analyze a word alphabetically and thoroughly sound it out, the next few times they encounter the word, it becomes easier to read.

After several successful readings of a word, two things happen. One, recognizing that word becomes automatic and easy, which expands the number of words automatically recognized and thus frees mental energy for concentrating on meaning. Two, the spelling and sound patterns of that word become part of a growing generalized understanding of the spelling/sound system. Thus, as this stage progresses, patterns of regularity for both simple letter/sound correspondences and other more complex patterns develop.

Consolidated Alphabetic Phase

As students become familiar with the richness and breadth of spelling patterns, syllables, affixes, and morphemes through extensive exposure to print and direct teaching, they begin to process larger units of print and read by analogy to known words—for example, recognizing the shared pattern in the words *rough, tough, enough* (Gaskins, Ehri, Cress, O'Hara, & Donnelly, 1996). This growing understanding of spelling patterns leads to the final phase, consolidated alphabetic, which begins in late first or early second grade (Ehri, 1995). As this phase progresses, students' increasing knowledge of larger units of print and their associated sounds accelerates decoding and leads to efficient reading.

In summary, every opportunity students have to successfully decode a variety of words advances the cause of their becoming automatic readers. The more sophisticated the tools beginning readers develop, the more text they can read and the more quickly they will become fluent readers.

Reading Instruction for Early First Grade

Research has provided a clear view of how best to help students become proficient readers. Effective instruction for early first grade focuses on the following elements:

- Knowledge of all letter names and shapes
- Full print awareness: Students can match oral words to printed words; identify the title and author of a selection; identify letters, words, and sentences
- More advanced phonemic awareness: Students can distinguish initial, medial, and final sounds in single-syllable words; distinguish long and short vowel sounds; recognize and produce rhymes; manipulate initial sounds to change words; blend two to four phonemes into recognizable words; segment single-syllable words into their phonemes
- The system of basic sound/spellings
- Decoding and word attack strategies: Students can generate sounds from letter patterns and blend those sounds into recognizable words, use letter patterns from known words to read new words, break compound words into two base words, recognize inflectional endings and root words, generate alternative pronunciations for ambiguous letter patterns (e.g., *bread*) and use context to confirm pronunciation, self-correct and self-monitor
- Recognition of common word families
- Knowledge of contractions
- Writing, spelling and dictation activities, and word play to reinforce and build on reading skills
- Automatic recognition of high-frequency words (both regular and irregular) and a growing number of other words
- Using syntax to aid comprehension, including the structure of sentences, clues from punctuation and capitalization, and anticipation of words
- Listening comprehension

* Reading fluency developed through rereading, auditory modeling, and oral reading
* Vocabulary and concept development
* Strategic reading
* Independent, wide reading and book discussions

Skills and strategies should be taught explicitly and directly, not as rote learning but in an active, problem-solving way. Students should be given ample opportunity to use them in reading for meaning with teachers, other adults, or partners.

Learning letter names and their shapes and print awareness was discussed in Chapter 3, "Beginning-to-Read Instruction for Preschool and Kindergarten." In early first grade, the other activities just listed should accompany continued instruction in listening to good stories and informational text and discussing their content, telling and retelling stories, listening to and singing nursery rhymes, giving explanations, and shared reading. These activities also should be dynamically related. For example, proficiency in letter/sound correspondences, phonemic awareness, word attack and self-monitoring strategies, word families, and automatic recognition of high-frequency anchor words each works in tandem to contribute to deciphering text. The more proficient a reader is in each of these areas, the better the chances are that a word can be read.

Furthermore, the best instructional methods will use one skill to develop the others. As one example, learning to recognize letter/sound correspondences enhances the latter stages of phonemic awareness, the ability to fully segment and manipulate phonemes; reciprocally, phonemic awareness activities can be used as a springboard to introduce the letters that match the target sounds. As another example, spelling and writing activities and the required attention to how print maps sounds are powerful tools in helping students learn the alphabetic principle.

Last, all these skills should help students develop a conscious understanding of the letter/sound system. Most top researchers and the best practitioners maintain that having active, thinking discussions with children—about connections, analogies, and comparisons of the details of the symbol/sound system and word attack strategies as students tackle print—is one of the most successful teaching techniques for developing students' ability to use these tools while reading (Marilyn Adams, personal communication, April 1995; Cunningham, 1990).

In summary, the purpose of teaching each of these components is to give students a high-powered repertoire of tools—recognition and decoding strategies—that helps them become automatic with increasing numbers of words and continues to develop their decoding skills, thus enabling them to read more and more text and become fluent with more words. Depending on the requirements of the text, the extent of the student's background knowledge, and his or her decoding skills, a particular student will use the various skills at his or her disposal in various proportions to decode the word in the most efficient and speedy manner. Thus, every student needs to be given the opportunity to learn the skills and strategies in each area and use them appropriately in decoding and reading for meaning so that he or she can learn to recognize a growing number of words automatically.

Joseph Torgesen (1995) writes that

> The self-teaching model of reading acquisition has at least three clear implications for teaching reading to young children that are not typically followed. First, it suggests the importance of direct instruction to help at-risk children acquire some reasonable level of alphabetic reading skills very early in the reading instruction process. Furthermore, the model shows why early acquisition of these skills is so essential: they provide the tools by which the child's subsequent experiences in reading text can contribute to the development of orthographic representations that are sufficiently specific to enable accurate distinctions between words during fluent reading. Second, the model suggests that there should be direct instruction to help children integrate the use of phonological clues and context in order to arrive at accurate pronunciations of words in text. Third, the model also shows why it may be very important to provide training in phonological awareness, either prior to or simultaneously with, early instruction in phonics and text processing. (p. 92)

Based on these ideas, we know early first-grade reading instruction should be organized around the following strands.

Completion of Letter Recognition and Print Concepts

At the beginning of first grade, students need to quickly develop full automatic recognition of every letter and complete print awareness. Most of these tasks should have been accomplished in kindergarten.

Phonemic Awareness Assessment and Instruction

First, students need to be assessed early for their phonemic awareness level, and an organized support program should be provided for those who score below the levels necessary to profit by phonics instruction. By late kindergarten to early first grade, all students should be able to identify spoken words that have the same first or last sound and begin to produce whole CVC words by orally blending the phonemes. Small group intervention should be provided if students haven't reached these important benchmarks. By early first grade, students also should be able to identify words with the same medial sound and be able to sound out a growing number of CVC words. The best way to ensure that all students stay on track is to provide dynamic instruction that uses students' growing phonemic awareness to explicitly teach sound/spelling correspondences in isolation and that provides repeated practice in blending previously taught sound/spellings into words. Second, the remainder of the students should increase their phonemic awareness through learning the sound/symbol system with the addition of some of the more advanced phonological manipulation and syllable comparison tasks (i.e., exactly how two syllables differ in phonemes; Lindamood et al., 1992). There is a strong causal and reciprocal relationship between learning to decode and developing phonemic awareness. Becoming proficient at one helps proficiency in the other and vice versa (Blachman, 1991, p. 11; Cunningham, 1990, p. 430; Share, 1995, p. 192).

One strong finding concerning the best method of teaching phonemic awareness—and actually any other skill—comes from a study by Anne Cunningham (1990) who contrasted ways of teaching two groups of first graders phonemic segmentation and blending tasks. One group just learned the tasks. The other split the time between learning the tasks and discussing and practicing how best to apply these skills. This second group was helped to reflect on and discuss the value, application, and utility of phonemic awareness—the students talked about how to use it in reading. Although both groups improved significantly in phonemic awareness compared to a control group, the group that received the conceptual or metacognitional level of instruction improved significantly more in reading comprehension (the skill-and-drill group improved to the 52nd percentile, whereas the metacognitional group improved to the 70th percentile; pp. 439, 441-442). Metacognition and conscious use should be built into any phonemic training strategy.

Benita Blachman (1991, pp. 16-18), who conducted the kindergarten phonemic awareness program discussed in Chapter 3, also developed a five-step first-grade program that illustrates how phonemic awareness training can support a beginning-reading program for children at risk of failure. The children in this program were some of those who had received the kindergarten program described earlier.

First, teachers reviewed the sound/symbol associations for a few minutes and introduced a new sound. Then, they emphasized phonemic analysis, using a Slingerland technique (named after one of the pioneers in teaching dyslexic children), in which a small pocket chart of letters, color coded for vowels and consonants, allows students to represent each phoneme in a word with its corresponding letter as the teacher pronounces it. After that, students would change the word to another word, such as *sat* to *sit* and engage in other word-building activities. In the next segment, these words were put on cards to be practiced for automatic recognition. High-frequency sight words were also introduced. This segment took a brief 2 to 3 minutes. The next segment was story reading, in which students tried to consciously apply the learned skills; this occupied most of the time. The program used phonetically controlled readers, stories from basal readers, and trade books. Last, there was a written dictation exercise of the words that had been produced earlier on the sound board and from the reading. Significant gains were produced compared to similar children who did not receive this program. Many new basal texts have incorporated these strategies into an organized program of systematic, explicit phonics instruction.

Instruction in Sound/Spellings

All students need a structured program that will give them the basic tools to decipher the English alphabetic system. Phonics instruction provides these tools by teaching the relationship between sounds (phonemes) and the spellings (graphemes) used to represent them and by teaching students how to use their knowledge of these sound/spellings and syllable patterns to identify written words. Knowing how to connect a printed word with its spoken form is a powerful tool: It enables students to develop automatic recognition of enough words to start reading, helps them decode new words, reinforces their understanding of how print maps to sound (the alphabetic principle), and further extends their phonemic awareness. Once students learn the 100 or so most common sound/spellings, they can learn many of the remaining correspondences on their own in the course of reading texts with minimal teacher support. Most students who possess little literacy preparation or who have auditory, visual, or memory problems need to continue a structured program for an extended period of time to learn the bulk of these correspondences. Other students will be able to learn the remaining correspondences fairly quickly through a more flexible program.

Learning the sound/spelling connections of the English language is much trickier than is commonly appreciated, for several major reasons. As Adams (1990) emphasizes, it is not just a case of teaching the letters and their corresponding sounds.

First, in English there is not a simple one-to-one correspondence between each letter and each sound. Because there are approximately 43 sounds and only 26 letters to represent them, sometimes a pair of letters maps to a unique sound (e.g., the consonant digraph *ch* in the word *chair*). There are also multiple letters (alone and in combination) that represent the same sound. For example, the sound /f/ can be spelled *f, ff, ph, lf,* or *gh*. Last, some letters are used to represent more than one sound. This is true of all the vowels and some consonants, such as *c* which stands for /k/ in *country* and /s/ in *city*.

Because of these multiple representations, there are hundreds of correspondence pairs in English, all of which eventually must be learned until they are securely lodged in memory and available for searching when a reader is trying to match the spelling patterns of the word being deciphered to the sounds of the word. Even when restricting the word universe to one- and two-syllable words found in reading materials of 6- to 9-year-olds, researchers found 211 sound/spelling correspondences. However, only 100 or so basic correspondences must be learned by the end of first grade. Many of the remaining correspondences can be learned independently by the maturing reader who knows how the sound system works and reads large amounts of text. Hanna et al. (1966) have identified the most frequent spellings of 43 English phonemes based on the number of occurrences in the 17,000 most frequently used single-syllable and multisyllabic words. (See "Sound/Spelling Percentages" in Resource A.) This information is useful in making decisions about which sound/spellings are important enough to teach and which, because of their lower-frequency, can be learned on an as-needed basis. Their findings show why the explicit teaching of about 100 correspondences covers all but extremely low-frequency patterns.

At the start, some of the common correspondences have to be directly taught, blended, used in reading, and checked. Older phonics programs moved very slowly through a structured approach to teach correspondences through the first and second grades. Adams (1990) found that these reading programs taught 170 correspondences by the second grade, at a rate of an average of 2 per week. The more effective, newer programs, some of which are described later in this chapter, are more accelerated for some children, use a greater variety of materials, such as trade books and multilevel reading materials written and adjusted for different rates of learning, and place heavier emphasis on independent reading.

Word Play and Word Work

Word work encompasses a range of activities that leads students to practice sound/spelling patterns by building, manipulating, and sorting words. In word building, students use magnetic letters or letter cards to make words dictated by the teacher. In the beginning, they should be given a small set of letters representing previously taught sound/spellings and asked to build words in sequence. For example, they might be given the letters *t, n, p,* and *a* and asked to make *tan, pan,* and *pat.* As students become more proficient, they can be given a larger set of letters to choose from. In *word sorting,* students sort words into categories based on sound and/or spelling patterns. Sorting activities are effective ways to reinforce the contrast between short- and long-vowel patterns. For example, students can be asked to write words or place word cards that have the same vowel sound under the key words *cat* and *cake.* After the sort is complete and they read the words aloud, they can do a second sort, grouping words according to specific spelling patterns and discuss the useful spelling generalizations they discovered (e.g., "The long-*a* sound can be spelled with *a*-consonant-silent *e* or with a vowel team."). *Words Their Way* (Bear, Invenizzi, Templeton, & Johnston, 2000) is an excellent resource for developmentally appropriate word work activities.

Writing and Spelling to Support Reading

Daily writing and spelling practice are essential in helping students develop their phonemic awareness and master the sound/spelling system. This practice includes assigned writing activities or writing as part of reading sessions (Foorman, 1995) and spelling words from phonics lessons and connected reading that contain the letter/sound correspondences being taught. Learning to spell a word correctly reinforces automatic recognition when reading.

Temporary or invented spelling (in which children approximate the spelling of words they hear or want to write) gives teachers useful information about students' grasp of particular letter/sound correspondences, their ability to segment words into sounds, and their understanding of the underlying structure of words. (See additional comments on invented spelling in Chapter 6). The *"Words Their Way Qualitative Spelling Inventory"* in *CORE Assessing Reading: Multiple Measures* (CORE, 2000) examines the types of errors students make and helps teachers select developmentally appropriate activities based on what students do correctly and on their invented spellings. Based on the results of the inventory, teachers can select activities that will improve learning and provide additional practice.

In first grade, students also should be learning to write brief narratives (e.g., fiction and autobiography) and descriptions of real objects, people, places, or events. Writing instruction should also focus on mechanics (such as punctuation and capitalization) and grammar and usage.

What Sequence?

As reasoned earlier, one of the major reasons to teach sound/spelling correspondences is to help students understand the idea that letters and letter combinations map to the sound segments of speech. Most will not understand this principle simply by being told it is true or even by being shown one or two examples. Many students will get the point only if they see example after example of this idea and are asked to think about the connections. Thus, it is important to first introduce students to those correspondences that are the cleanest and easiest to perceive, such as consonant sounds that relate to letter names (/s/, /l/, /m/) and the short vowels, and wait until later to teach potentially confusing alternative mappings. For example, although the sound of a long vowel is more obvious, whether or not a vowel takes that sound is complicated by which letter or letters follow it. That is why most code-emphasis or phonics-based strategies first teach the consonants, which can be demonstrated as the first or last sound of the word, and the short vowels. By focusing on consonants and a few short-vowel sounds early in the sequence, students can use their letter-sound knowledge to begin practicing building and reading CVC words.

Second, higher-frequency (and therefore more useful) sound/spellings should be introduced before less frequent ones; for example /m/*m* and /a/*a* before /j/*j* and /v/*v*. The third issue to consider is ease of articulation. Whereas students have a fairly easy time grasping the concept of an individual letter, the sound segments in speech are difficult to isolate or pronounce without adding another overlapping sound. Therefore, the first consonant sound/spellings taught should be *continuous sounds*, or sounds that can be pronounced for several seconds without distortion: /f/ *f*, /l/*l*, /m/*m*, /n/*n*, /r/*r*, /s/*s*. Blending the sounds of consonant *r* with the short vowel *a* and the consonant *n*, for example, makes it clear that each letter represents a distinct sound, and when they are combined, they form the word *ran*.

In contrast, try to say the phoneme represented by the letter *b:* It is impossible. You either say "bē" or "buh," both of which contain two sounds, which is why many children get confused when trying to blend the sounds of *bat*. They must learn to disregard as only an approximation the extra sounds in "buh" and "tē" to get *bat*. Teacher modeling and careful selection of words for blending practice can help students avoid confusion. Successful blending depends largely on word length and on the configuration of consonants and vowels within a word. Blending practice should begin with two- or three-phoneme words (VC and CVC) that begin with a continuous sound, e.g., *am, man*. Stop sounds, sounds that can be pronounced only for an instant, can be used in the final position: *at, map*.

Last, there is the problem of letters such as vowels that generate more than one sound. Think of all the different sounds *a* can stand for—/a/ in *at*, /ā/ in *ate*, /o/ in *watch*, /ə/ in *alone*, r-controlled /är/ in *far*, and so on. Adams (1990) recommends spacing the teaching of the alternative spelling/sound correspondences for a given letter over a period of time, when feasible. This way, the student learns the first correspondence well before the second is introduced, but it is not so set in memory that it fights against laying down the second alternative in memory.

There is a variety of recognized sequences of phonics that progress from the easier consonants and vowels, singly or in combination, to the more difficult ones. The different approaches possess some common attributes. All good programs will include the basic correspondences—the 21 consonants (including *y*); the short-vowel sounds of the five primary vowels found in most three-letter words (e.g., *hot, sit, bat, pet, cup*); consonant digraphs, such as /ch/ *ch* and /sh/ *sh;* long-vowel sounds spelled with silent *e;* initial and final consonant blends; endings such as *-ed* and *-ing;* r-controlled vowels; other vowel sounds, including vowel digraphs such as /ē/ *ea, ee,* variant vowel digraphs, such as /oo/ *oo,* and diphthongs such as /oi/ *oi, oy;* double consonants; silent consonants; common patterns, such as *igh;* beginning syllabication; and *el* and *le* in final syllables.

Most effective programs teach enough of each of these categories that children can learn the remaining phonic elements by themselves. How much is enough will depend on the child. Of course, the teacher must monitor the child's reading and fill in knowledge gaps in these correspondences after the child has completed this introductory stage. Many children need assistance well into the second grade; some learning disabled children need help for even longer. One can see the dilemmas teachers face in deciding how best to proceed, but any successful school must figure out a method and adopt materials that systematically ensure that each student eventually will become fluent with each of these correspondences.

How Much Practice?

For many children, both letters and letter combinations and their phonological correspondences are not easy to remember because they are confusing, abstract, and meaningless. To achieve a level of automatic recall and understand the system well enough to apply it to new words, they must invest a significant amount of time practicing recalling these combinations in a variety of reading circumstances.

For students who enter the classroom with a tremendous amount of prior experience with print, the initial symbol/sound lessons will be more review and clarification than introduction of new materials; that is, most will already know the sounds of consonants. The teacher can proceed fairly quickly to help those students perceive and become automatic in the overall system of the connections of letter patterns to sound. Because of their experiences with print, these students will also understand why the lessons are being taught and most will be highly motivated.

Students who have not had the background or who have visual, auditory, or memory processing problems must spend much more time on these lessons, including the reading of connected text with the teacher or receiving specially tailored instruction. This reality necessitates some differentiation of instruction or supplemental support from tutors or the teacher and aides. This is discussed later in this chapter.

If enough class time is devoted to learning these key letter/sound correspondences and other essential code-breaking skills and learning or reinforcing those skills in the context of reading appropriate stories, and if this skill instruction is followed by a significant amount of reading and teacher and classmate discussion, most students should learn almost all the phoneme/grapheme pairings thoroughly by the end of second grade, although some will not achieve this level until the third grade. Initially, the vehicle for instruction and follow-through should be materials designed specifically for or appropriate to these lessons. When students are capable of reading both narrative and informational trade books, magazines, and stories in textbooks, those materials should become the major—but not the only—vehicles to learn the remainder of these letter/sound correspondences, as well as to develop the ability to extend comprehension, discuss the stories or articles, and increase the number of books read.

A Major Caution About Letter/Sound Correspondences

If the English language mapped letter to sound as regularly as the Spanish language and had the relatively small number of distinctive syllable types of Spanish, then some of the potential confusions among students and the teaching profession would be avoided. One of the problems in teaching a whole set of possible sounds for a given letter or letter combination is that in learning this complicated array, both teachers and students often forget the purpose of the exercise. Its purpose is not just to generate alternative sounds for a given letter or letter combinations; it is also to assist students' mental retrieval systems by etching in memory more and more sound/symbol relationships. Then later, when looking at the letter patterns in a particular word, the reader can effectively search for the appropriate sounds that decipher that word and unlock its meaning so that the meaning of the word can be used in understanding the passage being read.

Furthermore, understanding simple letter/sound correspondences, although critical for becoming a proficient reader, is only one of the several mental processes necessary for automatic recognition of words. First, many words do not follow a one-to-one match of letters to sound and must be decoded by recognition of more complicated spelling patterns and sound relationships or by generating alternative pronunciations until one fits. Second, as explained previously, knowing letter/sound links is only one component of a series of complicated and dynamic mental processes triggered by attending to a pattern of letters. These processes interact simultaneously to conduct a search for the word stored in memory that matches potential combinations of the particular visual letter patterns in the word being read and the potential sounds associated with those patterns stored in memory. These processes search for likely word candidates and screen out unlikely ones, determine if any of the dwindling list of possible word candidates makes sense in light of what already has been read and the structure of the phrases and sentences of the passage, and last, make conscious the exact word that meets all the requirements.

The effectiveness and speed of this search depends on how well letters and letter patterns and the structure of the phoneme system have been incorporated in long-term memory, how practiced the reader is in using these systems in parallel, and how effectively the reader can use the meaning of what has been read so far to determine whether potential words would be appropriate. Relying on phonics instruction alone to carry the burden of developing facility in all these areas will not work. Instruction and practice must develop the dynamics of the total system.

Word Families

Students should learn to automatically recognize a growing number of key letter patterns or sequences that make up components of many words. Word families, or phonograms, are examples of these common sequences. The words *went, sent, tent,* and *spent* are part of the word family that shares the pattern *-ent* with the same final sounds. This shared structure is also known as a *rime,* or the vowel and everything that follows it in a syllable. Phonograms should never be the sole focus of early reading instruction because proficient word identification requires full sound-by-sound analysis (Bruck & Treiman, 1990). However, once students have been taught the sounds of the individual letters that make up a rime (/a/*a* and /t/*t*), they can be taught to blend the letters into a unit (*-at*)and then blend previously taught consonants together with the rime to form new words: *sat, fat, rat* (Ehri & McCormick, 1998). Teaching students to process larger units increases automatic word recognition. As many as 500 words can be derived from just 37 rimes (Wylie & Durrell, 1970), most of which should be recognized by mid-first grade. (Another approximately 200 regular rimes should be recognized by the end of first grade.) However, beginning-reading stories and materials must be designed specifically to highlight and reinforce these word-family relationships and organized so books are available to provide reading material for any particular word family being taught. Word building and word sorting also reinforce recognition of word families.[6]

Decoding and Word Attack Strategies

As previously discussed, the term *decoding* has been used in two different ways. The first definition is the ability to recognize a word instantly and effortlessly by a quick visual scan of its letter patterns (aided by context and syntax), which I refer to as *automaticity*. Instructional strategies that provide students with myriad opportunities to read individual words successfully numerous times will develop automatic recognition of an increasing number of words. The second definition is the more deliberate, conscious figuring out of a word not immediately recognized, by applying knowledge of the letter/sound mapping system. Such word attack proficiency is critical for two major reasons. First, the most effective way to become automatic with a particular word is to initially decode it—to consciously process both the letter patterns and sounds the first few times it is read. Second, because so many words important to meaning appear infrequently and because most reading materials will contain substantial numbers of new words, students need an effective system of decoding new words to have access to most materials.

Sounding out consists of looking at the letters or patterns of letters, knowing or approximating the sounds those letters represent, and blending together those sounds to make recognizable a word that is part of their speaking/listening vocabulary. This method is the most efficient mechanism to learn how to process new or not fully learned letter/sound combinations. Some students can handle previously unread words, finding it easy to apply their knowledge of letter/sound correspondences to sound out new words. However, a significant number need explicit instruction in sounding out words. Many students stumble in learning to decode because they haven't had enough practice blending sounds to read words that represent the particular patterns they have been taught. If students are to become independent readers of beginning materials by mid-first grade, learn to be self-teachers, and extend their reading abilities, they must have conscious command of several word attack strategies in addition to sounding out. These strategies include reading by analogy to known words, generating alternative pronunciations and using context to choose the right one, and recognizing larger chunks, such as base words and word endings.

An important point is that sounding out or any other word attack strategy does not have to generate the exact word but only get close enough so that the mind makes the right connection, much like placing a paper clip closer and closer to a magnet until it is caught. Sounding out a word also forces students to look at and attend to the spelling pattern in the word, a crucial step in laying down the retrieval patterns in their long-term memory, which will eventually result in automatic recognition of that word after several successful decodings. Thus, every successful incidence of sounding out a word reinforces visual identification and is one more step in achieving automaticity with that word.

As discussed earlier, many children who have had experience with print have memorized a significant number of words visually (without phonological recording), and by reading beginning material, they will memorize more. However, they cannot learn enough words in this manner to read the bulk of material they will eventually encounter, and retrieving the word from memory will also be slower than if they had phonologically recorded it.

Even in first- and second-grade materials, more than a third of the words occur only once; the majority occur five times or fewer. With so few learning opportunities, learning words one word at a time will not provide adequate growth in the students' visual vocabulary. Students must develop the ability to decipher unfamiliar written words through reading a large amount of material with those patterns and practicing with other reinforcement exercises. These activities will accelerate the recognition of those specific words and other words with related sound/spelling patterns. As a point of interest, most words read in first and second grade are already stored in memory as part of students' spoken language. Later on, readers confront the additional problem of deciphering a written word they do not know the meaning of, intuiting or learning that meaning, and installing that newly learned word in memory.

Very quickly, students encounter a major stumbling block in learning to read—many letter patterns have more than one pronunciation, and simple sounding-out strategies will not automatically generate the right candidate (the vowel team in *bread* can be pronounced with the short-vowel sound of *red* or the long-vowel sound of *reed;* or, more challenging, *react,* when first seen, could be pronounced "reeked," "wrecked," or "re-act"). Students must learn to generate legitimate pronunciation alternatives and use context clues to resolve the differences. David Share (1995) maintains that this difficulty is the "quintessential problem of reading acquisition" and that "independent generation of target pronunciations for novel orthographic patterns" is a critical skill in learning to read (p. 200).

In addition, through reading with the teacher or with partners, students should start to learn other strategic skills, such as thinking if they already know the word being deciphered or if it is similar to one they already have decoded; knowing how to break words apart into syllables and isolate word endings, such as -*ing;* reading in phrases; rereading; self-monitoring ("Can *duck* be the right guess for *bird* if the first letter of the written word has a /b/ sound and *duck* starts with a /d/ sound?"); and use of other graphophonic, semantic, and syntactic clues (Clay, 1991, pp. 237-345).

High-Frequency Words

A small group of words accounts for a large percentage of the words that appear in print. These high-frequency words are often very abstract but crucial for comprehension. They include words such as *the, of, to, was, for, at,* and *will.* Because fluent reading depends on the automatic recognition of these words, they are sometimes referred to as "sight" words. Some high-frequency words are completely regular, spelled with letters and letter patterns that represent their most common sound: *and, on, with, be, this, can.* Many, however, are irregular, with unique or infrequent patterns: *of, to, you, was, what, said, give.* Although students use these words in everyday speech, they would expect them to be spelled differently. Adding to the challenge is the fact that many high-frequency words are easily confused; for example, *was* and *saw* and *them, they,* and *there.*

By the end of first grade, students should be able to automatically recognize a pool of about 150 high-frequency words, including those that are regular. Students should continue to build on the pool of irregular words they learned in kindergarten, spelling them out letter-by-letter *before encountering them in text.* With this method, they have to attend to all of the letters, noting both regular and irregular patterns. This helps develop pattern knowledge, memorization, and automatic recognition. When students come across an unfamiliar word *during reading,* whether it has irregular spelling patterns or simply contains sound/spellings that have not yet been taught, they should use sounding out with contextual analysis to arrive at the pronunciation. This combination of phonetic decoding and use of context to verify fit and accuracy is a powerful tool given that so many words in English are off by only one letter/sound correspondence (e.g., *have, do, what*). Individual word banks and word walls are other useful ways to teach and reinforce students' recognition of high-frequency words.

Syntactic Awareness and Mechanics

To develop reading fluency and comprehension, students should be provided with further instruction in the structure of sentences, using clues from mechanics, such as capitalization and punctuation, and anticipation of words.

Listening Comprehension

During the important early first-grade period, it is essential for students to also hear good stories with new concepts, new ideas about the world, and new vocabulary. They need to participate in deep and extensive discussions about those stories to prepare them for the texts they will read. Even though development of listening comprehension is not essential to the first stages of reading—which depends on recognizing printed words already in the child's spoken vocabulary—listening comprehension becomes much more important in the second grade, and because growth of vocabulary and concepts takes time, these activities should not be slighted. Many students also need to develop a "sense of story" for their writing activities. This stems from exposure to engaging stories.

Fluency

Reading fluency is the rate and accuracy with which students read. Good fluency is the mark of a proficient reader who recognizes words automatically, groups them into meaningful phrases, and rapidly applies a combination of reading strategies to identify unknown words. It is to be expected that students' oral reading in late kindergarten to early first grade will be slow and labored because they are just beginning to "break the code" of written English. Toward the end of first grade, however, students should be able to read simple text aloud at a rate of 60 words per minute and in a way that sounds like natural speech (California State Board of Education, 1999). This is a sign that they can attend to the meaning of a passage as a whole rather than struggle with deciphering individual words.

Students become fluent readers by reading. The best techniques for developing fluency are independent reading and rereading of *manageable* texts; that is, texts that students are able to read with a high rate of success: decodable texts in the early part of first grade and beneath-frustration-level trade books from mid-first grade on. Some students fail to read fluently because they have never been exposed to fluent reading models. Auditory modeling through choral, echo, shared, and partner reading is another effective technique for developing proper phrasing, inflection, and stress (Allington, 1983; Dowhower, 1991). Readers Theater also can be used to develop fluency. "Rehearsals" provide an opportunity for rereading and peer and teacher feedback.

Fluency assessment should begin informally in first grade by listening to students reading aloud. At the end of first grade, students can be asked to do a formal timed reading of a short passage they haven't seen before. After the first unrehearsed timed reading, they work with the teacher to set a new target rate and then practice rereading the passage until they reach the target (Samuels, 1979). Repeated timed readings have been shown to improve not only reading rate and accuracy but comprehension and overall student confidence as well (Dowhower, 1987; O'Shea, Sindelar, & O'Shea, 1985; Trachtenberg & Ferrugia, 1989). (See Chapter 5 for information about using phrase-cued texts to increase fluency.) Motivation is important because poor fluency can become a self-perpetuating problem with struggling readers spending less time reading and reading fewer words than more able readers.

Vocabulary and Concept Development

Many first-grade students can understand and orally use about 6,000 words, but they have very limited reading vocabularies (Chall, 1987). (The English oral vocabulary of second language learners and children from low-income families is much smaller.) In first grade, instruction should focus on two types of vocabulary development: categorization of grade-appropriate concepts (e.g., animals, foods, etc.) and the words students hear and read that are crucial for comprehension. Direct instruction in specific words and concepts prior to reading helps students develop depth of word knowledge. This is particularly important for story-critical words that are conceptually difficult or that represent concepts that are

not part of children's everyday experience. The other important component of vocabulary development is instruction in independent word-
learning strategies that help students figure out the meanings of unfamiliar words they encounter while reading. Students can learn to look for
patterns shared with known words (e.g., the base word *play* in *playing,
playful, playground*) and to use context and surrounding text to help
them figure out the meaning of a new word.

.The majority of word meanings are learned through everyday experiences with oral language and print (Baumann & Kameenui, 1991),
including asking teachers, parents, and peers questions about word meaning. The best way to promote vocabulary growth is to increase the volume
of students' reading (Nagy, 1988). This, of course, depends on strong
beginning reading skills. Children can also learn new vocabulary by listening to Big Books and trade books read aloud if the teacher briefly stops to
define new words and models independent word-learning strategies.
Because multiple exposures are needed before students fully grasp new
vocabulary, teachers should point the words out in selections and ask students to use the words in their own writing and record them in vocabulary
notebooks. Teachers can also develop students' interest in words through
word play, humorous homophone books, Word-of-the-Day activities, and
"word detective" games (Cunningham & Stanovich, 1998; Graves, Juel,
& Graves, 1998).

For English language learners, the challenges of vocabulary development are even greater. Students have to understand the meaning of the
words they are asked to decode in order to store the complete amalgam of
information they need for automatic recognition. In addition to all of the
instructional components that have been described, they need added support: additional instruction time before and after school; preteaching of
vocabulary and concepts that may not be part of their linguistic or cultural
background; emphasis on meaning, rather than pronunciation; use of
pantomime, pictures, and graphic organizers to convey meaning; and
flexible grouping and smaller group size.

Strategic Reading

There are certain key comprehension strategies that students need to
master to become proficient, strategic readers (Pearson, Roehler, Dole, &
Duffy, 1992; Pressley, Johnson, Symons, McGoldrick, & Kurita, 1989).
For first graders, these strategies include using prior knowledge; under-

standing the structure of narrative (setting, characters, problem, events, outcome, theme) and expository text (e.g., time order sequence); predicting; identifying the main idea and summarization; responding to *who, what, when, where,* and *how* questions; using context; and visualizing. Instruction should help students understand *what* the strategy is, *why* it is important, and *how, when,* and *where* to apply it.

The are several reasons for poor reading comprehension: lack of automaticity with word recognition; limited vocabulary; poor syntactic knowledge; lack of understanding of text organization; lack of internalized reading strategies; and insufficient reading experiences. For students with limited word recognition and decoding skills, listening and responding to text read aloud is a way to expose them to a wide range of literature, familiarize them with different text structures, enrich their vocabularies, and develop their comprehension of *written* texts (Gillet & Temple, 1994). As students' reading abilities develop, the gap between their listening comprehension and reading comprehension closes. It is important to carefully select the texts used for comprehension instruction. When new strategies are introduced, familiar texts (e.g., folk tales and fairy tales) should be used, and when students practice these new strategies, it should be with texts they can easily read.

Retelling stories helps students understand what they read and develops their "sense of story" (Morrow, 1986). In retelling a story, students have to synthesize and organize information, make inferences, and draw on prior knowledge. In the beginning, retellings may be simple descriptions with a beginning, middle, and ending. As students become more competent readers, their retellings become more sophisticated, with information supplied through making inferences and explanations based on cause and effect (Brown & Cambourne, 1987). After teacher modeling and practice, students can retell stories to one another and use simple listener feedback forms.

Independent, Wide Reading and Book Discussions

Independent silent reading is one of the most important activities for the reading development of students of all ages. By reading on their own, they develop automatic recognition of a growing pool of words, independently learn the remaining elements of the letter/sound system, increase their fluency, develop vocabulary and comprehension, and become educated about the world (Shany & Biemiller, 1995). Wide reading also builds new background knowledge that helps them understand more complex content-area text. One of the best ways to motivate students to want to read is to have regular, classroom discussions about books. Discussions give students a chance to share their response to books, explore ideas, develop oral language, deepen their understanding of what they read, and learn about new books.

Independent reading and book discussions are integral to the literate environment that fosters strong readers. The goal is for students to read a half million words annually by fourth grade (California State Board of Education, 1999), and it takes careful planning to help students in first grade make progress toward that goal. The first step is creating a classroom library and arranging time for daily independent reading. Teachers can motivate students to read by reading aloud to them and helping them select books to read from classroom, school, and public libraries. Students should have access to a broad range of materials suited to their particular reading levels. Less able readers can be directed to books that have good picture/text correspondence, read with partners, and listen to an audiotape of a story as they follow along in the text. An optimum independent reading program includes 20 to 30 minutes of reading in class, plus 20 to 30 minutes outside class, for a total of 40 to 60 minutes daily. To be most effective, independent reading programs need to be implemented on a schoolwide basis through reading awards, contests, hallway displays, and community-sponsored programs (Center for the Study of Reading, n.d.).

Individual Diagnosis and Benchmarks: Keys to Effective Instruction

As discussed in the kindergarten section, instruction must be sensitive to the stages of literacy development and individual needs and thus must be diagnostically driven. Initially, that means assessing each student in the areas of phonemic awareness, reading comprehension, listening comprehension, word recognition, decoding, lexical or spelling knowledge, and concepts in print (Juel, 1994, p. 121).[7]

One effective organizational strategy is to observe children's efforts in these areas, assess their progress, and monitor each of them closely to gauge who is not progressing quickly enough. A teacher can then tailor programs from that knowledge. For example, if a student does not possess enough phonemic awareness to profit by phonics, he or she needs an organized intervention program and additional word and sound play and activities. A student who is not making progress on the Bryant or CORE ciphering test (using pseudowords) or a comparable test also needs special help. Alternatively, as discussed later, a teacher needs to keep a running observational record of how each child is reading or spelling, which mistakes he or she makes, and which self-correction strategies he or she uses. Instruction should reflect the differing and changing needs demonstrated by these ongoing assessments.

Combining Reading With Discussions and Feedback

One of the major dilemmas of the first-grade teacher is how to quickly and adequately prepare children to read trade books or stories in basal texts. As discussed earlier, after a short period of time, the strategy of just teaching letter/sound correspondences or memorizing sight words in isolation without trying to apply that skill in an actual reading situation becomes ineffective with many children. Many students get bored; they don't see the point of the exercises, and they stop trying.

More important, combining reading materials that reinforce and elaborate what has been taught in introductory lessons (connected reading) with discussions about how the sound/symbol and language structure systems work in the specific material read is one of the most powerful strategies for learning and reinforcing those skills and being able to apply those skills in the meaningful task of reading (Adams, 1990, p. 234; Foorman, Francis, Fletcher, Schatschneider, & Mehta, 1998; Juel, 1994, pp. 129-130). (Another essential strategy, writing and spelling lessons designed to reinforce skill lessons, was discussed earlier in this chapter.)

Furthermore, receiving on-the-spot feedback from the teacher, other adult, or student partner who assists the student in learning how to apply the skills and seeing the obvious link between learning phonics and reading text also enhances the effectiveness of phonics instruction. Connected reading provides the meaningful exercise necessary for linking spelling patterns with the rest of the cognitive system, whereas phonics without connected reading amounts to useless mechanics and is too easily forgotten. Discussion also gives teachers an opportunity to check comprehension. Students must practice integrating all the skills being learned in the actual act of reading for meaning—or, as in Michael Pressley's analogy, children who are learning to play baseball need to practice hitting and catching, but they also must learn to use these skills in an actual game (Pressley & Rankin, 1994, p. 166). Most important, reading should be fun. The earlier in their education that students can read a variety of high-quality books and materials by themselves or with a teacher, the more they will want to read.

On the other hand, reading for meaning cannot take place if the students are struggling over every word. A student who wishes to read a beginning book must have an already-developed critical mass of automatically recognized words and sufficiently honed decoding skills. Too many new words in a passage and underdeveloped decoding skills lead to frustration and discouragement. Furthermore, when too many words are unknown, students don't have enough mental energy left over after deciphering to attend to meaning. Students should use initial texts that provide them with high success rates in deciphering words. Clay (1991, p. 297) and Juel (1994, p. 122) state that for instructional purposes, students should be able to read at least 90% of the words, and for independent reading, they should be able to read approximately 95% of the words. Students need to be reading just at the level of being stretched so that they get enough practice in how the sound/letter system works, in learning new words, and in becoming more proficient in using cueing systems to read for meaning without becoming so frustrated that they lose focus.

Specially Designed Books and Materials

Decodable text, sometimes called "connected" text, is the intervening step between skill acquisition and the ability to read high-quality literature and informational texts. Decodable text contains three types of words: wholly decodable words, which can be identified on the basis of previously taught sound/spelling correspondences or phonic elements; sight words—high-frequency and story words that are explicitly taught to be recognized by sight as whole words; and nondecodable, noninstructed words that don't fall in either of the previous categories (Stein et al., 1999). Support for the use of decodable texts comes from comparative studies that show the efficacy of code-emphasis-explicit phonics programs (Adams, 1990; Anderson, Hiebert, Scott, & Wilkinson, 1985; Beck & Juel, 1995; Chall, 1987) and from basic principles of learning that dictate that instruction should provide students with opportunities to apply what they are learning in the context of use. Even common sense suggests that if the words beginning readers encounter don't conform to what they've been taught, they are not likely to be successful in their attempts at reading. Researchers have found that phonics lessons made little sense to children beginning to read if few of the words in their initial texts did not follow these regular letter/sound correspondences (Adams, 1990, pp. 276, 279-280). Faced with so many divergent patterns, many children become overwhelmed. To eliminate potential confusion and create successful reading experiences, we need to "simplify" the letter/sound system for children by using specially designed texts.

However, in the past teachers frequently encountered difficulty in finding books and materials that would reinforce the initial phonics lessons. Book publishers have begun to design more small books, stories, and reading activities that are aligned with the actual skills being taught. These books or materials need to be intrinsically engaging, and although they may include some more complicated words, they must also include a large percentage of words that correspond to the phonics and word attack lessons taught. Research has not pinned down the exact extent to which a text should be decodable to support learning. However, current state standards in California and Texas, respectively, call for 75% and 80% of the words in texts for early first grade to be *wholly* decodable. Obviously, whether or not a reading program's material meet these criteria depends on the particular program's scope and sequence of instruction. In addition, the notion of decodability shifts as students learn more about the letter/sound system. What was "nondecodable" in October becomes "decodable" later in the year.

These specifically designed or appropriate books should not constitute all the books or materials students read and discuss or that are being read to them. Connected decodable text materials are merely a portion of the total reading program—they play a particular role in late kindergarten to mid to late first grade. There are other criteria for selecting texts, such as the predictability and complexity of the language structure. Students need to hear and discuss a broad range of literature and informational texts.

An instructional strategy to avoid is one that provides for whole-class phonics lessons (especially when many students do not have the phonemic awareness to benefit from them) that are detached from reading and do not give students the opportunity to apply those decoding lessons in reading text. Juel (1994) looked at a group of students who, while still in readiness workbooks, were given whole-class phonics for 20 to 30 minutes a day. By November, the lessons had covered all 26 letters as well as 14 digraphs and blends—enough to read all 20 pseudowords on the Bryant decoding test. Children did not get to practice the lesson in specially designed materials and no check was made of phonemic readiness. This strategy proved extremely ineffective. The proportion of students who could pronounce a particular consonant in either initial or final position ranged from .37 to .67. Only about half the children learned each consonant. More damaging, the average score for correct sounding out of the 20 words was 6, with most children scoring 0 correct (Juel, 1994, p. 125). Phonics instruction without connected reading practice did not teach these students to internalize the letter/sound system.

Another misguided instructional strategy cited by Juel (1994) is the use of worksheets or workbooks with some groups of children while other children work with the teacher. First, these activities are also isolated from practice in actual text reading. Second, workbook assignments are usually not individualized; they are assigned whether the child knows the skill or not. Juel found few children needed help on letter recognition, yet they spent one third of their time doing worksheets on that relatively useless activity. Some children needed no help in any of the letter recognition, sight word recognition, and phonemic discrimination tasks. Yet they were still doing worksheets instead of reading for a purpose, as in class projects, participating in book clubs, or simply reading. Third, circling all of the same letters on a sheet does not help develop letter/sound correspondences or phonemic awareness because such work lacks an oral component. Children who can circle all the words that have the same beginning sound already have the skill (Juel, 1994, pp. 128-129). Although some tailored worksheet activities can be effective, uncritical, unguided use of worksheets to teach the complicated letter/sound and phonemic systems probably does more to discredit a skills approach than any other factor.

Correctness Versus Coverage

An important corollary of pitching the material just right is the necessity of pacing a student's reading to allow him or her to read every word correctly. One of Juel's most important findings was that students (all from low-income circumstances) who read the core basal text with 95% accuracy scored significantly above average on reading comprehension scores at the end of first grade, whereas all children who recognized less than 60% of the words of their basal text scored below the 38th percentile in reading comprehension (Juel, 1994, pp. 122-124). Amazingly, this relationship held regardless of the number of words read. Whether students read as few as 4,000 words in running text or as many as 31,000, the ability to identify individual words that had been read was more important than how many stories were read.

Juel (1994) explains that cipher knowledge determines first-grade comprehension, and if the child develops good cipher knowledge, it does not matter how many words are read. (This finding only applies to first grade. In later grades, the amount of text read becomes important, although correctness still matters. Thus, by second grade, both correctness and coverage count equally. As stated before, reading text helps lexical knowledge, which becomes more important in contributing to word recognition; listening comprehension becomes more important to reading comprehension; and extensive reading is the best way to develop those skills.)

Juel (1994) writes that

> Most children do not appear to gain cipher knowledge merely by seeing lots of words. First-grade teachers must make sure that children learn to read the words in their readers. Sheer coverage of stories will not compensate for, nor remediate, poor decoding skills. Quality of word recognition in first grade (i.e., being able to recognize words) is more important than quantity of exposure to words. On the other hand, once there is high-quality word recognition, then and only then does quantity of reading become critical. (p. 124)

The Importance of Timely, Early Intervention

During the past decade, schools have paid increasing attention to programs that provide rapid and early intervention or tutoring strategies for those students who are already slipping in the first grade because they are so deficient in skills. A successful reading program must have a strand that deals with this problem.

The best way to minimize the need for later remediation is to have good teaching in an organized program, clear benchmarks and interventions, and special support for those students who need additional help. (For critical literacy benchmarks, see Chapter 7.) In the early grades, frequent, ongoing assessment is crucial to pinpoint students' areas of strength and weakness and to guide decisions about grouping, pace, and intervention. There are several critical benchmarks during these years, including identifying the first sound in spoken words by mid-kindergarten, identifying the final and middle sounds by late kindergarten, and decoding simple CVC words by mid-first grade.

For struggling readers in the upper grades, assessment should pinpoint what is impairing their progress. If they do poorly on silent reading comprehension, they should be given a 1-minute timed oral reading fluency test. If students do well on the test, they would probably benefit from systematic instruction in comprehension strategies and may need testing to determine any gaps in vocabulary knowledge. If they perform below grade level in fluency, the next questions to ask are, "Is decoding a problem?" and "How much alphabetic knowledge does the student have?" Student performance on the *CORE Phonics Survey* (CORE, 1999a) points to four different levels of needed instruction. Some students can decode all of the single-syllable and multisyllabic words and are, therefore, ready to develop their strategic reading skills through independent reading of increasingly complex material. A large number of students do well decoding the single-syllable words on the test but have difficulty with the section on multisyllabic words. They benefit from several weeks of directed instruction in common syllable types and their division patterns—breaking words with two consonants in the middle between the consonants VC/CV (*kid•nap*) and reading words with the VCV pattern (which can break before or after the consonant) in the most typical way (V/CV with a long-vowel sound) and then using context to confirm pronunciation (*de•pend*). Another large group of students can only read words with simple linguistic patterns (e.g., CVC and CCVC words with short vowels and words with the VC*e* long-vowel pattern) but need directed instruction in the more complex vowel patterns and connected reading and writing practice. A fourth group is extremely confused and cannot read even basic CVC words. These students require further assessment to determine the cause of their difficulties and subsequent intervention in phonics and, if indicated, phonemic awareness.

Individual and Group Tutoring

In response to the America Reads challenge, across the country, many different after-school and summer tutoring programs have been implemented, with varying degrees of success. Some programs involve paid tutors, whereas others enlist the help of volunteers. If instruction is systematic and closely tied to classroom instruction, students do show some improvement (Allington, 1991; Slavin, Madden, Dolan, & Wasik, 1996). For example, Vellutino et al. (1996) provided poor readers in first grade with one-on-one tutoring in letter identification, phoneme awareness, word-reading skills, and practice with connected text. Daily 30-minute sessions were given for one or two semesters. The majority of the students became average readers.

Successful Reading Programs in the Classroom

Several examples of what effective instruction could look like in the classroom have already been outlined. In addition, some of the newest reading series and several successful reading programs incorporate effective skills strands along the lines discussed earlier.

New Series

Many new reading texts, particularly those developed for the California and Texas adoptions, reflect a balanced, comprehensive approach and use the powerful research on effective reading strategies and best practices. The programs include activities to develop phonemic awareness and provide systematic, explicit phonics instruction—direct instruction in basic sound/spelling correspondences, practice blending these sound/spellings into whole words, and connected reading practice with decodable texts. Unlike most reading programs of the past, current editions provide reading materials that are compatible with sequenced phonics lessons. New programs also use writing, spelling, and word work to build on and reinforce students' growing reading skills. Programs differ in the sequence of introduced sound/spellings and the pace of instruction. Some move children through very quickly so that the majority of sound/spellings are taught by mid-first grade and students can begin to read authentic texts. Others wait until late first grade or early second grade to complete instruction in basic patterns. Yet teachers should not impede students' progress by waiting to teach basic patterns such as *r*-controlled vowels and diphthongs. All of the basic sound/spellings should be introduced by mid-first grade. By the end of second grade, most new programs provide instruction in increasingly complex word attack skills, such as syllabication and morphemic analysis.

Publishers have responded to researchers and expert practitioners by helping teachers develop the foundation skills students need to read and respond to high-quality literature and expository texts. New programs expose students to a variety of genres and include instruction designed to foster vocabulary and concept development, syntactical knowledge, and strategic reading. Students are being encouraged to examine the structure of what they read, to reflect on aspects of its meaning, and to discuss its underlying message.

Although it is essential for educators to have good materials, successful implementation depends on two other crucial elements: training and leadership. Teaching staff and administrators must be committed to a schoolwide, collaborative effort. In *Teaching Reading IS Rocket Science,* Moats (1999) discusses the urgent need for teacher training and proposes a core curriculum that includes a thorough understanding of the structure of English (sound, spelling, meaning) and the use of teaching practices that are based on scientific research. She explains that "the demands of competent reading instruction, and the training experiences necessary to learn it, have been seriously underestimated by universities and by those who have approved licensing programs." Teacher training must go beyond workshops to include classroom demonstrations, professional coaching, and leadership training. For their part, administrators must take an active role in strategic planning—setting high standards, undertaking systemic changes, and creating an environment of inquiry and accountability. Since 1995, CORE has worked collaboratively with hundreds of schools to implement effective reading programs. Our success depends on schools assigning all necessary resources—people, time, materials, and funds—to support the mission of full literacy. This means releasing teachers for training and observation and administrators and lead teachers working together to ensure that good results are sustained over many years.

Grouping Strategies

Each school is faced with the reality that children enter first grade with widely different literacy levels and backgrounds. Schools cannot simply pitch their programs at those who have high levels of literacy training and let the bottom third fend for themselves. Unfortunately, too many schools, although giving lip service to the slogan "all students can learn," in reality allow many to flounder without a successful plan for improvement. Conversely, schools should not run all students through the same lockstep curriculum at the same pace if some students can proceed faster or already know the material.

What to do? Most successful programs around the country have developed a form of organizing instruction around skills levels for part of the reading period. For example, some reading programs initially recommend the use of partners and other skills-organized groups in first grade, then suggest breaking children into research groups of four to six for second grade.

Another effective grouping method is demonstrated by "Success for All." That program uses the Joplin strategy of reconstituting the primary grades into mixed-age classes, each with a specified curriculum, for 90 minutes of reading instruction appropriate to that group. The rest of the day is spent in heterogeneous grade-level classes. The reading classes are reconstituted every 6 to 8 weeks based on student progress.

Other programs organize five to six groups within the first grade to correspond to what children are learning and are careful to move children to different groups when warranted. They conduct many whole-class and other heterogeneous group activities. All these programs provide additional time for independent reading of the designed materials or anything else the student wishes to read, writing and spelling, conferencing, and a variety of other language arts activities.

Throughout the grades, the benefits of flexible grouping are obvious. It not only allows teachers to focus instruction on a group of students who share common learning needs, but it is the best way to closely monitor students' progress. Using this assessment, teachers can regroup students based on their current skill and knowledge levels. Skills-based grouping enables students to proceed at an appropriate pace through a sequence of well-defined objectives to meet grade-level expectations. For advanced learners, differentiated instruction allows them to work beyond grade-level expectations at an accelerated pace. Which grouping strategy is appropriate for a particular school or class will depend on the mix of children, staff preferences, and how many groups and how much flexibility a teacher can handle. However, every first-grade teacher must deal with the issue of varied literacy levels and preparation and make some flexible accommodation to be both fair and effective for all children.

Determining Structure

A related question concerns whether or not every child should be explicitly taught the same sequence of phonics and decoding skills. Some general principles point to the answer. First, as noted previously, there are a significant number of children, having either visual or auditory processing problems or few literacy experiences, who are going to need a long-term structured program. Second, every student needs some help in understanding how the total graphophonic, syntactic, and meaning system works, and each of them needs to be monitored for progress. All students' learning can be accelerated by a carefully organized program that systematically and sequentially introduces the most frequent sound/spellings. Some students work through the sequences rapidly, learn the concepts, and become ready for the trade books or basal stories in a few weeks. They quickly get the idea of and can recognize in print the letter/sound correspondence of a short *a* or even that the letter *c* can be soft or hard and what the pattern for each pronunciation is. However, most students take until December or January to reach this level. Others who have had little literacy preparation or have auditory, visual, or memory processing problems may take much longer. But every student must master this beginning sequence before moving ahead. Starting all students off with a systematic, explicit phonics program is the best way to ensure that they all develop the basic skills they need to become fluent, independent readers.

There are several drawbacks to teaching phonics *only* incidentally, on an "as-needed" basis. First, it is extremely difficult to plan a sequence of instruction based on utility and increasing difficulty if sound/spellings are introduced only as students encounter them in texts. Incidental instruction often involves an implicit approach that requires students to infer sound/spellings from reading whole words. This demands a degree of skill in both phonemic segmentation and making inferences that is beyond many students. When attempts are made to individualize beginning phonics instruction from the outset, classroom management also becomes problematic. Teachers who have a tremendous amount of experience will be able to juggle the large number of required strands and keep track of students in large classes so that they can effectively tailor instruction as the professional tutors do. Many of these teachers are currently achieving fantastic results and should not change what they are doing; they are already successfully integrating skills with the other strands.

However, this way of teaching is very complex and constitutes a stretch for most primary teachers who do not have the vast experience and training necessary to effectively operate such a strategically run classroom. These less experienced teachers need a basic organized program that has enough flexibility to be adjusted to different groups of children and that can be tailored to the individual students as the teachers become more skilled in these strands. (For a good discussion of this issue, see Pressley & Rankin, 1994, pp. 164-165.) Professional development investments aimed at helping primary teachers move up the professional spectrum are crucial to increasing overall reading performance.

Notes

1. Exposure to print also contributes heavily to lexical knowledge (about 50% in both first and second grades—the more students read, the more words they understand). There is one major caution about exposure to print in the early grades. It only works if the student actually reads the words correctly—making mistakes in a large number of words doesn't help (Juel, 1994, pp. 122-125).

2. Some decoding tests have been developed that use low-frequency *real* words, as opposed to pseudowords. In response to those who disagree with using pseudowords out of context as an assessment, the vast majority of the research community maintains it is the best measure of decoding ability and actually replicates what a student faces in seeing a new word. As Share and Stanovich (1995b) write, "We know unequivocally that less-skilled readers have difficulty turning spellings into sounds. This processing deficit is revealed by the most reliable indicator of a reading disability: difficulty in rapidly and accurately reading pseudowords [citations omitted]" (p. 7).

3. Juel (1994) cites similar results found by Lundberg in 1984 in Sweden, which starts children reading at age 7 (1 out of 8 chance for low phonemic first graders to become good readers by sixth grade) and by Marie Clay in New Zealand, which starts children reading at age 5.

> There is an unbounded optimism among teachers that children who are late in starting will indeed catch up. Given time, something will happen! In particular, there is a belief that the intelligent child who fails to learn to read well will catch up to his classmates once he has made a start. Do we have any evidence of accelerated progress in late starters? There may be isolated examples which support this hope, but correlations from a follow-up study of 100 children two to three years after school entry lead me to state rather dogmatically that where a child stood in relation to his age-mates at the end of his first year at school was roughly where one could expect to find him at 7:0 or 8:0. (Juel, 1994, p. 120)

4. According to Share and Stanovich (1995b),

A phonemically segmented lexicon (words placed in memory by their letter/sound patterns) in conjunction with the ability to supplement a not-yet-completed decoding with contextual information may permit the reader to achieve early 'closure' thereby easing the memory burden in decoding and reducing the likelihood that prior sentence context will be lost as a consequence of slow and inefficient word identification.

5. For the point that just because students find it more and more difficult to memorize increasing numbers of words, they won't necessarily switch to an alphabetic decoding strategy, see Share and Stanovich (1995b), p. 20.

6. There is some dissent on whether word families should be taught as part of early beginning reading instruction. See the research cited pro and con by Share and Stanovich (1995a).

7. Juel (1994) used the Roper/Schneider oral test for phonemic awareness—early first grade; the Reading Comprehension Test of the Iowa Test of Basic Skills (appropriate for end of first grade), the WRAT reading subtest for word recognition, the Bryant Diagnostic Test of Basic Decoding Skills for cipher or decoding knowledge, the Spelling subtest of the ITBS for spelling or lexical knowledge, and the Metropolitan Readiness test for early first grade.

5

Reading Instruction for Middle First Grade to Upper Elementary Grades

A Book- and Story-Driven Strategy to Teach Skills

Once students possess the skills to read simple trade books, stories, children's magazines, and informational text from beginning anthologies, one of the most effective skills development strategy is to use these materials as the vehicle for extending the number of words that can be recognized automatically and perfecting the ability to use phonics knowledge to decode words. If it takes several trials to move from sounding out a word to automatic recognition, then the more times a student reads a particular word, the more automatic he or she becomes. Most students become automatic with a word after recognizing it successfully 4 to 15 times. Some students, as they become more proficient, can recognize a word automatically after two or three tries. However, many children with learning disabilities need to read a word in context as many as 50 to 100 times before it becomes automatic.

As students learn to recognize more varied patterns of words, they establish more comprehensive letter/sound correspondences and spelling, syllable, word family, and word-root patterns in memory. They are then able to learn to recognize new words more quickly. Reading a variety of materials also should sharpen decoding skills and enable students to learn new words and develop automatic recognition of high-frequency words (many of which have irregular spelling/sound patterns) as well as the 300 word families that make up the 1,500 frequently used words in primary children's vocabularies (Adams, 1990, p. 321). These materials should be read as part of independent and teacher-directed reading activities aimed at extending reading capabilities and opening up doors of knowledge, enrichment, and joy for children. Direct teacher instruction should continue as a supplement to this strategy, especially in the area of the more complex decoding skills that depend on knowledge of advanced letter/sound correspondences, syllabication, word structure, spelling, and mechanics. Books should include both literary (stories based on narrative comprehension) and informational (based on expository comprehension, such as in science, history, or biography) texts.

As students read with partners or in groups, they can discuss content or even reading strategies. Furthermore, the teacher can model word and text analytical skills, such as awareness of language structure, recognizing word similarities, or understanding textual organization. Students should read large amounts of increasingly complex materials (with more difficult vocabulary and a greater conceptual load) to use and sharpen the growing number of skills they have learned. As in the pre-trade-book stage, school or classroom programs can be organized in different ways to accomplish these tasks, but each successful program must face the same instructional challenges—helping students perfect their decoding skills, grow their vocabulary, learn syllabication and morphemic analysis, and become strategic readers.

First Principle: Match Books
to Students' Levels

Classrooms should be filled with good children's literature appropriate to the various students' reading capabilities. This will take additional resources, but it is one of the best investments a school or district can make. Students who can decode well need more challenging materials and need to increase the amount they read, as the amount and level of reading becomes the strongest determinant of future growth. Juel (1994) found that for students scoring in the top quartile in reading comprehension at the end of first grade, almost all second-grade improvement in comprehension resulted from amount of text read. Conversely, as discussed earlier, if students have not yet mastered the sound/symbol system, coverage is less important than correctness.

All students should be reading just at the level where they can be extending their reading knowledge. If they are reading books and recognizing 98% to 100% of the words, they are not going to progress because they have no opportunities to practice decoding and learn new vocabulary; conversely, if they cannot recognize at least 90% of the words and do not slow down to read each word correctly, the materials are too difficult for learning to occur.

Reading series offer a graduated variety of text. There are several ways to measure text difficulty. Books at the lower levels use a high percentage of words containing previously taught letter/sound correspondences, few words per page, simple sentence patterns, oral versus literary language, many supportive illustrations, and consistent placement of print. The upper-level materials use conventional stories, literary language, specialized vocabulary, more sophisticated language structures with oral language appearing in dialogue, challenging vocabulary, and few illustrations. These levels include familiar children's literature or informational books in areas such as science, history, and biography. Most students should reach these levels by the spring of first grade. Children eventually must read a tremendous amount of material, after they crack the code, if they are going to be grade-level readers by third grade and graduate from elementary school reading grade-appropriate materials—about 100 to 200 little books during the first grade and about 25 to 35 grade-equivalent fiction and nonfiction books a year starting in late first grade.

Once children can read more sophisticated classic and contemporary children's literature, nonfiction informational materials, and school texts in other subject areas, these materials can be used as the basis for assigned readings to generate more profound discussions about what has been read. Materials above students' reading levels should be read to them with follow-up discussions. Assignments in class can be oriented more to projects and activities that necessitate research or reading for a purpose. These types of activities should already be a staple of classroom organization.

Second Principle: Frequently Evaluate Students' Reading

It is essential that most of what students read is challenging enough to develop their automatic word recognition, vocabulary, and skills but not so hard that they become frustrated. Student background knowledge plays a role in this equation. This includes what they know about the letter/sound system and also their knowledge of the content (topic, genre, author), the vocabulary used, and the text organization. As stated, a good rule of thumb is that if students cannot automatically recognize at least 90% of the words, they will become frustrated; if they sail through, recognizing 98% of the words, they are missing an opportunity to extend their word learning. (This formula does not mean students should never read an interesting book if it is too hard or too easy; rather, that a steady diet of either extreme will cause problems.) Students should be recognizing approximately 95% of the words automatically, which means they are decoding (in the sense of figuring out) about 1 word in 20. This requires teachers to keep tabs on how each student is doing. Frequent conferencing and having the child read to the teacher are important components of any successful reading class.

Oral reading fluency is an excellent way for teachers to gauge what materials are appropriate for independent reading. If students are able to read aloud at an even pace with few errors, they are likely to remember and understand the text. Reading simple text aloud in a way that sounds like natural speech is an important benchmark that students usually achieve toward the end of first grade. The primary strategy for developing fluency is to provide extensive reading opportunities with manageable texts: familiar, predictable texts and decodable texts in late kindergarten, decodable texts in the early part of first grade, and beneath-frustration level trade books from mid-first grade on.

Informal assessment of fluency usually begins in first grade with teachers listening to students read aloud. Formal timed tests can be given at the end of first grade and repeated periodically between grades 2 and 8 to measure students' progress. These tests involve unrehearsed readings of two to three brief grade-level passages. Teachers count the number of words students read correctly in one minute. They can then use students' average WCPM (words correct per minute) to rank their performance based on oral reading fluency norms developed by Hasbrouck and Tindal (1992). As mentioned previously, the California framework calls for students to be reading 60 WCPM at the end of first grade. The mastery targets are about 78 WCPM by mid-second grade, about 93 WCPM by mid-third grade, about 112 WCPM by mid-fourth grade, and about 118

WCPM by mid-fifth grade. If students fall below the established fluency norms, decoding is usually implicated. As explained earlier, an assessment of decoding, such as the *CORE Phonics Survey* (CORE, 1999a), will help to pinpoint the cause and inform instruction. Some students will need instruction focusing on multisyllabic words; others will need instruction in reading single-syllable words with the more complex letter/sound correspondences, and still others will need instruction in the most basic elements of the system.

Decoding may not be a problem for some students who fall below the established fluency norms. For these students, the starting point of intervention can be rereading practice with partners; listening to live or audiotaped modeling of fluent reading; timed repeated readings of the same passage until they reach a desired target rate; and practice with phrase-cued, or segmented, texts. Practice with text that is marked to show the natural pauses within and between sentences helps students who have good word recognition but who need help grouping words into meaningful phrases and whose oral reading is choppy and monotone. (See the *CORE Teaching Reading Sourcebook* [Honig et al., 2000] for more information about oral reading fluency norms, curriculum-based measurement, teaching strategies for developing reading fluency, and intervention for struggling readers.)

Many existing practices for grouping violate the principle of matching reading materials to individual needs. First, assignment to large reading groups or whole-class instruction means that only some children have appropriate materials. Most often, the group is paced by the best readers, and the others do not have a chance to accurately read each word (Juel, 1994, p. 127).

Second, districts and principals often pressure teachers to cover an established amount of material. Groups may start slowly but accelerate and lose children. In Juel's (1994) study, the pace speeded up when the group reached the primer stage, and by February, students were recognizing only 66% of the words. Rather than slow down, reread, or use similar techniques, the group simply forged ahead. By June, word recognition was still only 69%, and reading comprehension was only at the 29th percentile. (Recall that if basal texts were read at a slower rate with at least 90% correctness, comprehension scores were way above average [p. 127].)

Third, in most classes there was very little regrouping even if a student was reading with extremely high accuracy. Unfortunately, second-grade placement often was made not on ability but on a student's last reading-group assignment. Most effective programs reconstitute reading groups every 6 weeks or so.

Last, allowing a great deal of free reading results in students picking books significantly below or above their reading level. Considerable effort on the part of the teacher is necessary to keep children in the right books. In their report, Ronald Carver and R. Leibert (1995) found that a significant percentage of the books picked as grade-appropriate material for fifth graders were actually at third-grade level (p. 43).

In summary, when readers read easy books, they do not encounter the new vocabulary and more sophisticated ideas necessary for growth. Conversely, when poor readers pretend to read, or any readers continue to struggle through, books significantly above their abilities, they will become frustrated—unless, of course, their proficiency accommodates quickly to the harder material by their learning the specific vocabulary and ideas of the topic covered by the book.

One of the most needed tools for teachers is a uniform standard for determining the grade level of a book—not as an average in a nationally normed test but as a measure of difficulty appropriate for a given grade. In the past, teacher judgment and library lists with broad ranges (e.g., third to fifth grade) had to suffice. A major breakthrough has occurred with the development of the Lexile Analyzer by MetaMetrics in Morrisville, North Carolina. They have created a proportional scale and software that can place a book on the scale based on the number of infrequent words occurring and the amount of internal text references (phrases and clauses). They have ranked over 3,000 children's and adults' books and materials. For example, *Cat in the Hat* is ranked 200; *Goodnight, Moon* is 300; *Charlotte's Web* is 800; *The Adventures of Tom Sawyer* is 1,000; *USA Today,* 1,100; *The Wall Street Journal,* 1,400. The highest level is George Washington's Inaugural Address, at 1,700. Lexile rankings can be used starting in late first to early second grade. Reading at a 500 lexile level means that a student can get 75% of comprehension questions correct on material at that level. (The scale is logarithmic, so that being at 500 means that a student will get only 50% of comprehensive questions right at the 700 level, and this relationship holds throughout the scale. The Lexile Analyzer software will rank any book or any student.)

Continued Phonics, Spelling, and Decoding Support

As discussed previously, students in middle first grade are still at different levels of proficiency in decoding, phonemic awareness, and word attack and strategic reading skills. Teachers need to provide ongoing support in these areas until the students have learned the letter/sound system completely and have mastered more complex decoding and word attack skills. As soon as students are able to read CVC*e* words, teachers can model breaking compound words into two known words, looking for simple inflectional endings, such as *-es* and *-ing*, and dividing words with the VCCV syllable juncture pattern (e.g., *rabbit* and *basket*) between the consonants (Chall & Popp, 1996). Instruction in spelling, which also contributes significantly to reading improvement, should continue throughout the elementary years. Spelling instruction is discussed in detail in the next chapter.

Multisyllabic Word Instruction

Marcia Henry, Carrol Moran, and Robert Calfee make the important point that one of the prime difficulties of reading English is the complex nature of breaking words into parts (see Henry, Calfee, & La Salle, 1989, p. 155 et seq.; Moran & Calfee, 1993, pp. 210-212).

For students in second grade and beyond, knowing how to decode unfamiliar multisyllabic words is crucial because most of the new words they encounter are "big" words. Some students intuitively transfer their phonics knowledge from single-syllable to multisyllabic words. Many students, however, become overwhelmed by long words, unable to break them down into smaller parts. When good readers encounter a long, unfamiliar word, they assign it a pronunciation by chunking letter patterns into manageable units (Adams, 1990; Mewhort & Campbell, 1981). In the early stages of reading development, these units may be recurring phonograms (e.g., *-ill, -ack*) or inflectional endings (e.g., *-es, -ing*). In later stages, students begin to recognize larger units, drawing on their knowledge of which letters "pull together" in syllables (e.g., *dr*) and which "pull apart" into separate syllables (e.g., *dn*).

Syllabication instruction helps students tackle multisyllabic words by teaching them how to recognize the various syllable types and their pronunciations, identify syllable junctures and their division patterns, and use what they know about morpheme units (common prefixes, suffixes, and root and base words). To decode multisyllabic words, students must also have the necessary "mental flexibility" to break a word into syllables, come up with approximate or alternative pronunciations, and then use context to confirm the word and, if necessary, change the pronunciation.

There are six basic syllable types in English. The most common are *closed syllables,* in which a single vowel is followed by a consonant and the vowel sound is usually short (*picnic*), and *open syllables* that end with a single vowel and usually have a long-vowel sound (*veto*). To identify *r*-controlled and *vowel team* syllable types (e.g., *corner, cowboy*), students train their eyes and ears to recognize that two letters remain together as a unit producing a single vowel sound. To identify the *vowel-silent* e syllable type (*lifetime*), students recognize the silent e as a marker that indicates the preceding vowel sound is long. The sixth syllable type is *consonant*-le. Students can be taught to count the number of consonants that come before *le* to help them determine if the preceding syllable is closed with a short-vowel sound or open with a long-vowel sound (*little* vs. *title*).

Learning about syllable juncture patterns helps students know where to divide a word and how to pronounce it based on the resulting syllable types. For example, the world "moment" can be divided mom•ent and pronounced with a short "o," or it can be divided after the "o," which makes the "o" long. In English, about two thirds of VCV words break after the vowel and a third after the consonant so it is important that students learn to try to break new words both ways.

The common division patterns are VC/CV (*bas•ket*), V/CV or VC/V (*mo•ment, plan•et*), VC/CCV (*mon•ster*), VC/CCCV (*in•stru•ment*), and V/V (*re•act*). Beginning in second grade, teachers can show students how to physically mark syllables by labeling all the letters that make a vowel sound, then labeling the consonants between the vowels, and finally marking the syllable divisions with a slash. These marking procedures help make the underlying word structure transparent. With practice, students will be able to identify the syllable types on their own, recognize consonant digraphs and blends, and arrive at an approximate pronunciation.

Nagy and Anderson (1984) found that learning the structure of words at the syllable and morpheme levels improved students' word recognition, spelling, and vocabulary knowledge. Nagy has stressed the point that English becomes increasingly morphologically complex in the texts used in upper grades. He noted that students must learn huge numbers of complex words and that one of the difficulties they face is the tendency of many word roots to change spelling and pronunciation in different word forms; for example, the root *photo* breaks differently in the words *pho•to•graph* and *pho•tog•ra•phy*, with resulting changes in vowel sound. Understanding the history of English helps in understanding the structure of words because each contributing language has its own peculiar pattern of letter/sound correspondences, syllabication, morphemes, and word generation.[1]

For example, the majority of everyday compound words are of Anglo-Saxon origin. Words such as *football* were made by combining two other words. Words derived from Latin and French tend to be more technical, formal, or literary, such as *manuscript, facilitate,* and *international.* Many words, such as *traction,* were created by adding prefixes or suffixes to a word root that usually cannot stand alone. Greek-derived words, such as *biology* or *astronaut,* are found primarily in technical fields and are specialized.

In summary, it is also important to help students become aware of units of meaning and the more complex syllabication patterns as the words they encounter become increasingly multisyllabic. According to reading experts, students need to learn about the underlying structure of words in our language to become proficient readers and writers. Knowing the different patterns and roots becomes essential as material increases in difficulty. There are three layers at work in English orthography: the alphabetic layer, the pattern layer, and the meaning layer. A proficient reader uses all of these layers to figure out how to decode a long, unfamiliar word. As early as second grade, students can be taught an effective four-step strategy for reading big words: (a) Look for familiar word parts (prefixes and suffixes) and cover them. (b) Look for familiar vowel and consonant patterns in the base word. (c) Divide the base word into syllables. Sound out the syllables and blend them to say the word. (d) Uncover the word parts and blend the whole word. You can see how well this strategy works by trying to decode the following sentence: "The traphestal difference between the bafister jacepot and the torquial wexid lies in the function of the dighton" (Gross-Glenn, Jallad, Novoa, Helgren-Lempeses, & Lubs, 1990). Even without any context, most proficient readers will be able to decode the nonsense words and pronounce them in a very similar way.

Note

1. For three fascinating accounts of the historical basis of the creation of English and the many linguistic streams that feed into it, see Bryson (1990), Claiborne (1983), and Crystal (1995).

6

Spelling, Beginning Writing, and Vocabulary

Spelling

Spelling and beginning writing are essential components of any successful reading program in kindergarten, first grade, and beyond. As mentioned earlier in the kindergarten section, learning to print letters obviously helps a student recognize them. Beginning writing and spelling activities that have students attempt to translate spoken words to written words (encoding, which is the converse of decoding) help reinforce the letter/sound system. Subsequently, an organized spelling program is essential for first through eighth grades and should aim toward making students good spellers with good spelling habits.

The Importance of Spelling

Because spelling requires an understanding of how letters and letter patterns map to sounds, poor spellers are often poor readers. Learning to spell a word correctly reinforces automatic recognition because all of the graphemes become embedded in the reader's mind and get attached to sound and meaning. Researchers, including Bear (1991), Ehri (1992), Gentry (1998), and Henderson (1981), have found a significant correlation between children's spelling knowledge and their reading speed and accuracy, comprehension, pronunciation, and vocabulary and concept development.

Fluent spelling skills also are crucial for effective communication. When students continue to struggle with the mechanics of writing, they aren't able to focus their attention on what and why they are writing (Harris & Graham, 1996). Donald Graves (1994), one of the most respected leaders in the writing reform movement, makes these comments about the importance of spelling:

> Spelling does matter. It matters far more than we in the profession realize. Spelling, probably more than any other aspect in the school curriculum, is used to mark social status. . . . Spelling matters for another reason. Children who initially write down words using inventions or temporary spellings are establishing their learning habits and attitudes towards words and writing. As arbitrary as spelling may appear, specific things should be taught and certain attitudes established. It is not enough for the writer to know what the text says. As Mary Ellen Giacobbe points out, the reader needs to know as well. Writing is communication. (pp. 255-256)

Temporary or Invented Spelling Issues

In many schools, students begin writing before the formalized reading program starts, and writing becomes a powerful tool in developing skills and knowledge about reading. "Invented" or "temporary" spelling is a technique that allows students to approximate the letter and patterns of letters that represent a given sound and so permits the construction of more advanced writing connected to student interests. It is a helpful technique for encouraging students to write, and it pays off in increased writing volume and more elaborate stories, which in turn encourage children to think more about what they are writing than do traditional techniques. Temporary spelling also helps with understanding the phonics principle.

Adams (1990) points out that the payoff for students who have had ample experience with temporary spelling is in spelling growth and reading fluency (p. 383), but she warns against the tendency of some programs to teach phonics through spelling. Encouraging writing using temporary spelling cannot replace instruction and practice in reading and word recognition. She argues that direct instruction in word analysis and consonant blending is a necessary complement to children's independent orthographic intuitions (pp. 378-388).

The issue of how best to correct temporary or approximated spelling is somewhat controversial. On the one hand, in preschool and kindergarten, invented spelling is a natural stage in developing the ability to write and spell, and teachers should allow room for natural child development and approximation. After kindergarten, writing (encoding) is used not just for expression but also as a powerful technique to help children learn the letter patterns necessary for automatic decoding. At this stage, developmental spelling becomes an important diagnostic tool for determining how much progress the student has made in learning the sound/symbol system and what further instruction needs to occur. For example, writing *sumtime* for *sometime* shows good phonic skills and understanding of English spelling patterns, whereas *smtym* is much less developed.

Many teachers wonder when they should begin giving feedback about invented spelling and demand correctness. According to Bear et al. (2000), "The answer is: right from the start. Teachers must hold children accountable for what they have been taught. What they haven't been taught can be politely ignored." Because phonics and spelling instruction are sequential and cumulative, there will always be some features of English orthography that have not yet been taught, so students will "invent" an approximate spelling. Beginning in mid to late first grade, teachers should require that all words be spelled correctly in final drafts of writing assignments. This conveys the message that correct spelling is valued and helps students develop good spelling habits.

Stages of Spelling Development

Children learn to spell in a predictable series of developmental stages (Bear et al., 2000; Beers, Cramer, & Hammond, 1995; Henderson & Templeton, 1986; Moats, 1995). In each stage, they use invented spellings that reflect their current understanding of English spelling rules and patterns. These temporary spellings are not random, but rather change as students' orthographic knowledge grows. For example, a child's spelling of the word *dump* is likely to evolve from "d" to "dp" to "dop" or "dup" and finally, to "dump" (Bear et al., 2000). As students mature in their spelling development, they draw on multiple logics, including knowledge of syllable types, word structure (inflectional endings, affixes, and roots), visual features (length, letter order, patterns), and parts of speech and meaning. Although visual memory plays a part in spelling, orthographic knowledge is mostly a matter of concept development.

Determining Stages of Spelling Development

Students grasp spelling patterns and principles at different rates—even within a given classroom, teachers see a wide range of achievement. There is now wide agreement among experts in the field and experienced practitioners that spelling instruction must be individualized—linked to each student's stage of linguistic development. Otherwise, students become frustrated trying to memorize words they are not ready to learn. This is what happens when students seem to "know" a word on Friday and forget it on Monday. The goal is for students to develop lasting insights into how the writing system works.

To plan effective instruction, teachers need to assess how students are progressing in their spelling knowledge and select words and patterns for study that are neither too advanced nor too easy. (See the section later in this chapter on choosing words for spelling lists.) Samples from daily writing assignments are a good starting point. In addition, formal inventories can be given at regular intervals throughout the school year. Bear et al. (2000) have developed different versions of the *Words Their Way* "Primary and Upper Elementary Spelling Inventories." The *CORE Assessing Reading* uses the original versions developed in 1996. These inventories are easy to use and are designed to provide a sufficient sampling of invented spellings. Gathering invented spellings from both formal inventories and writing samples enables teachers to compare a student's performance in different contexts.

For each developmental stage, teachers need to examine what students do correctly, what they use but confuse, and what is absent in their spelling (Invernizzi, Abouzeid, & Gill, 1994). Instruction should focus on what students use but confuse; for example, if teachers find that a student is overgeneralizing the use of the vowel team *ee* to spell the long-*e* sound ("meel" for *meal*), they know that the student is ready to learn the different patterns for long-*e* in CVVC words.

Teaching Spelling

During the late 1980s and early 1990s, many schools moved away from formal spelling instruction. This was in part a reaction to the traditional drill-and-skill approach and its emphasis on rote memorization. It was also due to a widespread belief that students would learn to spell "naturally" by being immersed in reading and being asked to proofread their written work. Yet research has shown that experience with reading and writing does not guarantee that students will learn to spell. Conversely, without an organized, sequential program of instruction, those students who are the least able readers will not learn the orthographic patterns of English and, therefore, continue to struggle in reading. In places where teachers stopped providing formal spelling instruction, reading test scores dropped, and schools began to experience failure with literacy instruction (Ehri, 1992; Hughes & Searle, 1996; Peters, 1985; Treiman, 1996). There is now widespread consensus that for many children spelling is not *caught*—it must be *taught*.

Being a good speller is within almost everyone's reach, because spelling vocabularies of only about "3,000 words are sufficient for fluent and intelligent communication for adults" (Woloshyn & Pressley, 1995, p. 116). Fifty words account for half of written material and 1,000 words account for 95%. A small number of words—about 300—account for more than half the words children misspell in their writing. Although English spelling is complex, there are patterns, principles, and rules that actually make it quite orderly and predictable (Foorman, 1997; Moats, 1995; Venezky, 1970). The goal of instruction is to help students discover and internalize these patterns and features.

A marked shift in spelling should occur in late first or early second grade. By that time, children should have progressed from using only salient sounds to a phase in which they try to match a letter for each sound and are now ready for the more complicated orthographic learning necessary to become proficient at spelling. To become good spellers, they must graduate from relying only on sounding-out strategies to the more complex spelling-pattern stage based on orthographic patterns and word roots and incorporating a variety of more complex strategies in learning to spell a word.

To help develop good spelling habits and spelling consciousness, teachers need to convey the message that spelling matters. As discussed previously, this begins with the expectation in first grade that students will produce polished and correct final drafts. Beginning in second grade, students can take an active part in their spelling development by correcting their own weekly pretests and using the results to plan their weekly word study. At the end of the week, they can correct their posttests to gauge their progress. Another way to develop spelling consciousness is through self-diagnosis. Students can work with teachers to examine, diagnose, and correct the spelling errors in their written work. Errors tend to fall in four categories: (a) those made because of the way students pronounce the word ("git" for *get*), (b) those made because students wrote the letters out of order ("reprot" for *report*), (c) those made because there is more than one way to represent a given sound ("chane" for *chain*), and (d) those made because of a lack of knowledge about English spelling rules and generalizations ("storys" for *stories*). If teachers see that students' errors fall into a particular category, they can teach students useful self-monitoring tips. For example, if students consistently write letters out of sequence, they should be encouraged to say the word the way they spelled it to see if it sounds right.

In addition to developing good spelling habits, best practice

- Individualizes instruction by linking it to students' stage of development
- Actively engages students in discovering spelling patterns
- Provides students with opportunities to apply what they have learned to reading and writing

Which Strategies?

From kindergarten through eighth grade, 12 to 15 minutes per day should be devoted to spelling instruction. In kindergarten and first grade, students can do a variety of hands-on activities that will build their conceptual understanding of how the writing system works. These include building words with letter cards, as described in Chapter 4, doing picture sorts, drawing and labeling, word hunts, and word games. From second grade on, students can be given a weekly pretest made up of developmentally appropriate words. After they correct their tests and identify the words and patterns they want and need to learn, they should use a technique to help them store the visual image of each word in long-term memory. One proven technique, based on the work of Ernest Horn, involves six steps: (a) *Look* at the word, (b) *Say* the word, (c) *Cover* the word and *see* it in your mind, (d) *Write* the word, (e) *Check* your spellings, and (f) *Rewrite* the word correctly.

Word sorting is useful across the developmental continuum beginning with what Bear et al. (2000) calls the "letter name" stage. Researchers found that word sorting activities improve students' ability to spell words and to read them as well (Hall, Cunningham, & Cunningham, 1995). Sorting words by sound and spelling patterns helps students see similarities and differences among words and discover important concepts, including the connections between spelling, pronunciation, pattern, and meaning (Zutell, 1998). Starting at the end of the letter name stage, each student can keep a personal word study notebook. They can use the notebooks to record the words in their sorts and the spelling generalizations they discovered; list spelling "demons" and tips for remembering how to spell them; do word hunts in trade books and content-area reading; play word games; and write sentences, paragraphs, and stories using the words they are studying. The end-of-the-week posttest can include words for review, words with the target patterns (including those they missed on the pretest), and new patterns that students will be studying next.

Many educators have moved away from the traditional approach of teaching spelling "rules." However, there are some spelling generalizations that are useful to know because they apply to many words (e.g., rules for forming plurals, rules for adding suffixes and inflectional endings). Bear et al. (2000) explains that the best way for students to make sense of how words work is by discovering consistencies and making generalizations themselves rather than being told to memorize a list of rules. The teacher's role is to organize instruction so that these rules become explicit and to get students in the habit of "looking at words, asking questions, and searching for order."

Which Words?

Learning words in lists is more efficient than learning to spell individual words presented in context. There are several things to keep in mind when evaluating the lists of commercial spelling programs or creating new word lists for spelling instruction. First, the words should be linked to students' individual developmental levels. For example, for students in the early stage of within-word-pattern spelling, the word lists should focus on long vowel patterns found in CVVC words (e.g., *rain, tail, paint, straight*) and CVCe words (e.g., *bake, place, grade, change*). Second, the words on the list should be high-utility words grouped by pattern and presented in a systematic sequence. Lists should include words for review that students consistently misspell, including "demons" such as *their, about, too,* and *would.* Last, the lists should include words from content-area reading and literature that fit the pattern(s) being taught but should avoid words that are uncommon or unusual because the goal is to help students develop useful spelling strategies and to apply generalizations based on known words.

Grouping words by sound pattern introduces students to a large number of words to use when they need to write an unfamiliar word with the same sound. As an alternative, word lists can be composed of words that have the same visual pattern with different sounds (e.g., *tough, thought, through*). This is a way to help students remember the visual form of a word—an important key to being able to spell it. Another way to group words is by meaning pattern (e.g., *teach, teacher, teaching* or *please, pleasant, pleasure*). This helps students focus on the meaning layer of English orthography and develops the important strategy of figuring out how to spell unknown words by thinking of their meaning relationship to known words.

Some of the new basal spelling programs meet the criteria outlined here. There are several other good resources for spelling word lists. These include *In Other Words: A Resource of Word Lists for Phonics, Spelling, and Vocabulary Study* (Ganske, 1996); *The New Reading Teacher's Book of Lists* (Fry et al., 1995); *The Scholastic Rhyming Dictionary* (Young, 1994); and *The Spelling Teacher's Book of Lists* (Phenix, 1996).

Beginning Writing

In first grade, writing depends two thirds on the ability to spell words and one third on the quality of and ability to produce story ideas, including planning, reflecting, and revising (Juel, 1994). By second grade, these two factors have reversed. Spelling ability is determined by two main factors in first grade—cipher (or decoding) knowledge and lexical or memorized spelling patterns for that word. Both these factors decrease by second grade but still account for the majority of writing ability. Thus, first-grade writing is affected by some of the same factors as reading. (In first grade, writing ability is highly correlated with word recognition, and reading comprehension becomes increasingly correlated with writing ability as the grades progress.) It is apparent not only that learning to read helps learning to write and vice versa but that low phonemic awareness that inhibits decoding also stymies writing growth.

Juel (1994) and her fellow researchers devised a nine-point writing scale and then did backward mapping similar to what they did in reading by looking at which factors seemed to make a difference. Poor writers either spelled poorly or generated poor ideas. If a child was a poor reader, the odds were that the child would also be a poor writer by the fourth grade, and the correlation between reading ability and writing ability increased each year. This seemed partly explained by the influence of oral storytelling ability—a major determinant of the idea side of writing—and exposure to expository (nonfiction) text. No poor reader could score higher than 4 out of 9 levels on a basically expository fourth-grade prompt.

It is interesting that all first graders scored about the same on Juel's (1994) writing scale measure, but the good readers who encountered increasingly sophisticated stories as they were exposed to print increased significantly in the next three grades, whereas the poor readers stayed flat. As a result, a significant gap opened up by fourth grade. Juel explains that early reading ability affects the desire to read, which affects the amount of exposure to print, which affects later reading, writing, and speaking ability (p. 48). See chapter 8 for a discussion of writing standards and curricula.

Vocabulary

After decoding ability, vocabulary acquisition is the most important factor in reading comprehension. Clearly, students cannot understand what they read without knowing what most of the words mean. Research by Anderson and Freebody (1981) revealed that the proportion of difficult words in text is the single most powerful predictor of text difficulty, and a reader's general vocabulary knowledge is the single best predictor of how well that reader can understand text. Particularly in the upper grades, not understanding one word can prevent students from understanding an entire passage. Therefore, the automatic recognition of a growing number of vocabulary words is crucial to understanding the increasingly difficult text that students encounter as they progress through the grades. To begin to fully appreciate this task, consider the number of words used in the English language. According to McCrum, Cran, and MacNeil's (1986) *The Story of English,* "The statistics of English are astonishing. Of all the world's languages (which now number 2,700), it is arguably the richest in vocabulary." The *Oxford English Dictionary* lists approximately 500,000 words, and another half million technical and scientific terms are not catalogued. In comparison, German has a vocabulary of about 185,000 and French fewer than 100,000.

As far as school texts are concerned, our best estimate is that roughly 88,500 word families appear in books used through twelfth grade (Nagy & Anderson, 1984). About half of the texts we read, however, consist of the 107 most common words, and another 5,000 words account for an additional 45%. This means that 95% of the texts we read consist of approximately 5,100 words (Adams, 1990). Thus, the remaining 83,000 words or so, which carry most of the content, occur in only 5% of texts. Another way to look at the amount of vocabulary growth that is necessary is to consider that average second-grade students have a reading vocabulary of about 2,000 to 5,000 words, yet the materials they will read in third through ninth grade contain approximately 90,000 different words (Graves et al., 1998). Thus, according to the best estimates, students need to learn approximately 3,000 to 4,000 words per year throughout their school careers just to stay on grade level. Given that children learn between 5% and 10% of previously unknown words from a single reading, the only way to ensure that they will learn this mass of crucial yet low-frequency vocabulary is through adequate exposure to text in the form of wide, independent reading. This is the basis for the California State Board of Education's (1999) recommendation that student's in the early grades read 500,000 to 1,000,000 words per year.

Effective Vocabulary Instruction

As explained previously, the single most important thing teachers can do to promote vocabulary growth is to make sure that students read a large volume of text in the classroom and at home. A schoolwide independent reading program is essential. In addition to acquiring new word knowledge through reading, students of all ages learn new vocabulary by listening to texts read aloud and getting instant feedback to their questions about word meanings. There are three other components of effective vocabulary instruction: teaching independent word-learning strategies, providing specific word instruction, and fostering word consciousness.

Independent Word-Learning Strategies

Because students learn most new vocabulary through reading, they should receive direct instruction in a set of strategies that will help them learn word meanings independently (Kameenui, Dixon, & Carnine, 1987). These independent word-learning strategies are using word parts, using external context clues, and using dictionaries and other reference aids:

Using word parts: Analyzing the internal structure of words by looking for prefixes, base words, compound words, and Greek and Latin word roots. Students should learn the meanings of useful word parts—the common prefixes *un- re-, in-,* and *dis-* and the suffixes *-less* and *-ful*—and be shown how they can use these meanings, together with the meaning of the base word, to figure out an affixed word, such as *disbelieve* or *hopeful.*

Using external context clues: Hints provided by the surrounding text, including semantic devices, such as direct definitions or explanations, examples, restatements, and comparisons or contrasts. According to Anderson and Nagy (1991), because most word meanings are learned from context, the main focus of vocabulary instruction should be teaching students how to decode an unfamiliar word and then use context clues to determine its meaning.

Using dictionaries and other reference aids to confirm and deepen knowledge of word meanings. Traditionally, vocabulary instruction has focused on having students look up words in the dictionary and using the information in the definitions to write sentences. However, this has often resulted in students quickly forgetting a word or gaining only a superficial understanding. With appropriate instruction, using a dictionary can be a powerful aid to word understanding. First, teachers need to model how to look up the meaning of an unknown word and choose the definition that fits the way the word is used in a particular context. The most useful dictionaries provide sentences that clearly illustrate a word's meaning in context. Many advanced dictionaries also give useful information about synonymous terms, explaining nuances and gradations in meaning among terms such as *eat, consume, devour,* and *feast.*

When modeling these three independent word-learning strategies, teachers should select text with familiar content, limit unfamiliar words to a manageable number (about one every two or three sentences), and choose target words that are of high utility and within students' readability level. Providing students with their own vocabulary notebooks for recording new words and their meanings also supports students' independent word learning.

Specific Word Instruction

Direct instruction in specific words is another way to contribute to students' vocabulary development by increasing the depth of their word knowledge (Nagy, 1988). The intentional, explicit teaching of vocabulary is particularly important for words that are conceptually difficult or that represent complex concepts that are not part of students' everyday experience. Each week, teachers should select two or three words to explore in depth and devote 20 to 30 minutes of class time to each word. Specific word instruction is also useful for helping students understand key vocabulary in upcoming texts. Preteaching words before reading is especially helpful for English language learners who have a more limited listening and speaking vocabulary, may not be familiar with the concepts presented in the text, or who may not be able to use syntactic clues to figure out word meaning (Bernhardt & Kamil, 1998).

Vocabulary development is a complex process in which students draw on prior knowledge, use context, apply their knowledge of how the English language works, and use their general cognitive ability. Research has shown that effective instruction uses a variety of techniques to help students make connections between unfamiliar words and their prior knowledge (Stahl, 1999). These techniques include asking students to categorize and classify words, develop a semantic map, make a synonym web, or complete a semantic feature analysis grid that compares and contrasts the features of words in a category. There are several other proven methods for teaching word meaning, including possible sentences (Stahl & Kapinus, 1991), concept of definition map (Schwartz & Raphael, 1985); word analogies (Gillet & Temple, 1994); and the PAVE procedure (Blachowicz & Fisher, 1996). The keyword method was originally developed to teach vocabulary to second language learners and later adapted for use as part of first-language vocabulary instruction (Levin, 1993). It has also been shown to be especially effective with students who have learning difficulties (Mastropieri, Scruggs, & Fulk, 1990).

In selecting words to teach prior to reading, teachers need to consider how important a word is to the particular selection and how useful it will be in future reading. The first step is identifying the words in the text that are likely to be unknown or difficult for students. Students themselves can be quite accurate in rating their word knowledge, so teachers can list the potential vocabulary words and ask students how much they know about each one (White, Slater, & Graves, 1989). The next step is to make a revised list based on students' responses. The final step is identifying those words on the revised list that are the most important to teach. The following questions can guide teachers' decisions (Graves et al., 1998):

* Is understanding the word crucial for understanding the main ideas in the selection?
* Is direct teaching necessary, or will students be able to identify the word's meaning using context or structural analysis?
* Would direct instruction in this word enhance students' use of context, structural analysis, or dictionary skills?
* Will knowing the meaning of this word be useful in future reading?

Word Consciousness

Students who are word conscious are interested in words, understand the power of words, and enjoy learning new words. Teachers can foster word consciousness by reading aloud and discussing examples of vivid language, modeling adept diction, encouraging frequent use of the thesaurus, and by creating "word-of-the-week" and "find-the-best-word" activities. Golick (1987, 1995); Scott, Hiebert, and Anderson (1994); and Watts and Graves (1995) have written about using games to teach word histories, shades of meaning, and adroit usage. Activities with homophones, puns, eponyms, borrowed words, and onomatopoeia are excellent ways to generate interest in the remarkably rich lexicon of English. The goal is for students to experiment with new words in their writing and speaking as they develop a deep appreciation for the power of language and the importance of precision.

One of the most grievous deficiencies in most elementary classrooms is the absence of any formalized vocabulary attention. Several of the better vocabulary programs are listed in *Teaching Vocabulary to Improve Reading Comprehension* by William Nagy (1988), *The Nature of Vocabulary Acquisition* by Margaret G. McKeown and Mary E. Curtis (1987), *Teaching Vocabulary in All Classrooms* by Camille Blachowicz and Peter Fisher (1996), *Teaching Reading in the Twenty-First Century* by Michael Graves, Connie Juel, and Bonnie Graves (1998), the chapter on vocabulary by Michael Pressley and Linda Lysynchuk (1995) in *Cognitive Strategy Instruction that REALLY Improves Children's Academic Performance,* and *The Vocabulary Conundrum,* by Richard Anderson and William Nagy (1992).

7

Comprehension and Assessment

Good readers begin with attention to the word and then add their stored knowledge to weave strings of words together into a meaningful whole. This requires that they recognize and access the meaning of each word as rapidly and effortlessly as possible—automaticity—and that they consciously apply specific strategies that help them make sense of what they are reading—strategic reading. Researchers have found that comprehension is an interactive process, in which readers think about what the author is saying and connect it to their prior knowledge (Anderson & Pearson, 1984; Pearson et al., 1992). This background knowledge includes prior personal experiences; knowledge of the topic, the text structure, and the key concepts and vocabulary; syntactic knowledge; and the readers' understanding of how print works and how letters and letter patterns map to sound.

There are three main strategies for developing students' reading comprehension:

- Ensuring that students read a large amount of text
- Explicitly teaching comprehension strategies and text organization
- Engaging students in deep discussions about books

Independent, Wide Reading

The best strategy for developing comprehension is for teachers to require students to read a significant amount of age-appropriate, quality material. *"Reading a lot" is one of the most powerful methods of increasing fluency, vocabulary, and comprehension, and becoming educated about the world* (Shany & Biemiller, 1995; Stanovich, 1993a).

Growth in comprehension depends on reading a substantial number of words each year from a variety of high-quality children's literature and informational texts, such as favorite stories, children's newspapers, science and history books, biographies, and so on. A goal of 25 to 35 grade-appropriate fiction and nonfiction books from accepted lists seems right for most children. This will ensure that they are exposed to an adequate number of words to develop their vocabulary, as explained in the preceding chapter.

There are two main rationales for this recommendation. First, comprehension cannot improve unless the student is increasing the number of words that can be recognized and understood automatically. Shu, Anderson, and Shang (1995) cite numerous studies that show a high correlation between vocabulary growth and increases in reading comprehension (pp. 76-86). Getting meaning from text depends on first deciphering a word until it is conscious, understanding the concept embodied in that word, and then relating that word to other words in the sentence. At first, students know most of the words encountered in text; they need to recognize that the letters on the page represent a word they already know. Soon after the early primary years, however, students need to learn a substantial number of new words if they are to understand grade-level material. These words usually are the key to understanding the meaning of a passage. Eventually, students will need to learn to automatically recognize these words to stay at grade level.

Average fifth-grade students encounter about 36,000 new words per year in the course of their reading. Because students remember about 5% of new words encountered in context, a student reading average amounts will learn only about 1,800 words a year, not enough to keep up with needed vocabulary development. They must read more text if they are to extend their vocabulary (see Adams, 1990, p. 149; Anderson, 1992; Juel, 1994, p. 120; Krashen, 1993; Pressley & Lysynchuk, 1995, p. 102).

Thus, by the fifth grade, if elementary students want to make grade-level progress, they should be reading more than 1.1 million words a year of outside-school reading (25 to 35 books or the equivalent), which should take 15 to 30 minutes a night; this is in addition to the 1.7 million words in school text. Instead of reading the necessary 2.8 million words, the average fifth grader reads only about 900,000, and the bottom third read 1/10 or less the number necessary to stay at grade level. They fall further behind each year. Current U.S. students read much less than they once did—which is one reason reading scores are dropping—and much less than students in other countries. Although teaching vocabulary strategies helps retention rates, the vast majority of new words *can be learned only through reading.* To reach these levels, students need to read the recommended 25 to 35 books a year after the first grade.

A second rationale for this instructional strategy is that reading a large amount of material provides students with a broad and deep encounter with ideas, concepts, and knowledge. This, in turn, helps improve their ability to comprehend. By reading a variety of age-appropriate material from accepted lists, students should become more educated about the personal, social, literary, political, ethical, and scientific worlds. Becoming more literate is desirable on its own merits, but because background knowledge has a major influence on comprehension, being well-read contributes significantly to the ability to comprehend a wider and more difficult amount of written material.

Individualized Reading Program

Educators need to develop an organized individual reading program for each student. This strategy requires the following elements:

- A targeted number of books to be read from acceptable lists (both fiction and nonfiction)
- A variety of available books in the classroom and school library that are suited to individual students' independent reading levels
- A mechanism for checking that the books have actually been read, and a method of matching book to student
- A motivational strategy; teacher conferencing with three or four students during sustained silent reading allows students to share their responses to what they have read and provides an opportunity for teachers to recommend new books based on students' interests and abilities; an excellent way to pique students' interest is to preview new titles by reading aloud the first chapter and discussing it

▪ A record that travels with students throughout their school careers tracking all of the books they have read, so that teachers can identify any gaps in their reading experiences

Requiring a specific number of books to be read and keeping track of them is probably the easiest and most productive reading program a school could undertake. Parental involvement in the process—setting time aside for reading at home, discussing the book with a child, looking at the reading record—can greatly assist in attaining this goal. Every elementary school in the country should institute this program.

Strategic Reading

In the past few decades, researchers have examined what proficient readers do to construct meaning from text. Their findings reveal that able readers make conscious decisions, selecting *comprehension strategies* that fit the kind of text they are reading and their purpose for reading it (Anderson et al., 1985; Pearson et al., 1992). As explained previously, these key strategies include using prior knowledge, predicting, identifying the main idea and summarizing, questioning, making inferences, and visualizing. Students' awareness and understanding of *text organization* also plays a key role in comprehension (Dickson, Simmons, & Kameenui, 1998). Text organization encompasses both the physical presentation of the text—headings and subheadings, signal words, location of main-idea sentences, and graphics—and the underlying text structure, which usually falls into the broad categories of narrative and expository text.
According to Adams (1990),

skilled readers characteristically pause at the end of major syntactic units to wrap-up and assure themselves that everything is making sense; if the interpretation of the just-read clause requires inference or complicated pronoun references, the wrap-up is significantly increased. (p. 186)

This syntactic awareness is a special challenge for English language learners, even those who are able readers in their primary language and have learned other comprehension strategies. As they progress with decoding and word attack skills, it is their lack of vocabulary and the complex nature of English syntax (e.g., conjunctions, complex sentences, and dependent clauses) that becomes the greatest obstacles to reading comprehension (Bernhardt, 1991).

Comprehension Strategies Instruction and Metacognitive Knowledge

The goal of comprehension strategy instruction is to help students become interactive readers who monitor their own comprehension and apply and adapt a set of effective strategies to increase their understanding. Teachers can help children develop their metacognitive skills by asking questions such as "How did you know that?" and "What do you do when you come to a word or a part of a story you don't understand?" (Irvin, 1998). To encourage students to "think about their thinking," teachers also can model self-monitoring techniques, such as adjusting reading speed, rereading, reading on, and checking understanding after reading.

Most students require explicit instruction in reading comprehension strategies (Tierney, 1982). The teaching model that has grown out of recent research emphasizes teaching students *how* and *when* to use a strategy in the context of authentic reading tasks. Although strategic reading must be fluid and flexible, students should be aware that some strategies are better suited to certain parts of the comprehension process—those used in preparation before reading, those used to increase the effectiveness of reading, and those used to increase their recall (Pressley & Woloshyn, 1995). When modeling new strategies, teachers should use narrative and expository texts that students are familiar with and select texts for strategic reading practice that students can easily read.

Effective strategy instruction includes direct explanation, modeling, guided practice, feedback, and application to other texts (Dickson, Collins, Simmons, & Kameenui, 1998). There are several proven methods that combine these elements. One of the earliest, reciprocal teaching, was developed by Brown and Palincsar (1984).

The technique uses guided instruction to help students generate questions about the upcoming passage, clarify word meanings or confusing text, summarize the passage read, and make predictions about the next passage. Another feature of reciprocal teaching is its use of scaffolding. Initially, the teacher assumes control as discussion leader, guiding students in applying the comprehension strategies and providing feedback. Over the course of several sessions, the teacher gradually releases responsibility to students. A review of these techniques showed significant gains of about a third of a standard deviation on standardized tests and .88 standard deviation on researcher-designed comprehension tests (the research reviewed included older students; Rosenshine & Meister, 1994).

Pressley and his colleagues have also thoroughly discussed the benefit of strategic reading for the development of comprehension ability and the ability to extract the gist or macrostructure of what has been read (Pressley et al., 1992; Pressley & Rankin, 1994, p. 159; Pressley, Symons, McGoldrick, & Snyder, 1995). They advocate programs for Grades 3 through 8 (some strategies are appropriate in earlier grades) in which teachers use strategies to assist children in making mental associations between what they have read and their own personal experiences, interpreting them, and creating summaries of what they found important in the text.

DRTA (directed reading and thinking activity) and QAR (question-answer relationships) are two other effective instructional strategies. In a DRTA, students take part in a predict-read-prove cycle to set a purpose for reading, process ideas, and cite text that supports their predictions (Stauffer, 1975). QAR was developed by Taffy Raphael (1982) to help students understand the three-way relationship that exists among a comprehension question, the text to which it refers, and the reader's prior knowledge. Again, a gradual-release format is used, with the teacher initially modeling QAR concepts and terminology over the course of several lessons.

Text Organization

Understanding how text is organized helps readers construct meaning (Dickson, Simmons, et al., 1998). Most *narrative texts* are organized around a set of common elements—setting, characters, plot, and theme—known as *story grammar.* Comprehension instruction begins with narrative text because by the time most children enter school, they are already familiar with stories that have a beginning, middle, and ending. Making students aware of story grammar gives them a framework for constructing meaning and provides an anchor when they are listening to stories, retelling them, and eventually writing them on their own. In kindergarten, students can use simple story maps to identify the setting and characters and the beginning, middle, and ending of a simple plot and then use the completed maps to orally retell the story. Starting in first grade, students can use more detailed story maps, with the added elements of problem, outcome, and theme.

Whereas narrative text tells a story, *expository text* provides an explanation of facts and concepts. Its main purpose is to inform, persuade, or explain. As students progress through school, they devote most of their reading time to textbooks, articles, and other expository texts. Their success or failure in school, therefore, is closely tied to their ability to understand, learn from, and remember the information presented in expository texts. Some of the materials students read are "considerate," providing visual clues that direct readers to the concepts and ideas that are central to comprehension. Headings and subheadings function as a map of the main ideas. Topic or main-idea sentences provide readers with a framework for understanding and recalling important information. In addition, writers use key words, such as *because, unlike, most important,* and *before,* that signal the relationship among ideas and point to the internal organizational pattern—cause-effect, problem-solution, compare-contrast, description, or time order.

To help students recognize and use visual textual clues, starting in kindergarten, teachers can read aloud big books and explain tables, charts, and maps that expand on the ideas presented in the text. In first through third grades, students should learn how to use tables of contents, chapter titles, headings and subheadings, and charts and graphs to locate and recall important information and to understand how ideas are related. Developing an outline or written summary helps students clarify, comprehend, and recall what they read. Starting in second grade, students can begin to use the main idea (explicitly stated or their own) and supporting details to write a summary of short passages and eventually an entire selection.

K-W-L (Ogle, 1986) is the most well known and most frequently used technique for dealing with expository text. The basic process involves three steps: recording on a chart What I Know (accessing prior knowledge), What I Want to Know (setting a purpose for reading), and What I Learned (recalling what has been read). Carr and Ogle (1987) expanded the process for older students, adding two final steps: concept mapping to group text information and summarizing. Teachers should show students how to use the physical features of text to fill in the chart. Graphic organizers are another effective technique for increasing students' understanding of text organization (Wood, Woloshyn, & Willoughby, 1995). Teachers can model filling out graphic organizers with formats that are appropriate to the text structure of a particular selection; for example, a time line for a text written in time order sequence or a problem → action → result chart for a selection that describes a problem and solution.

Book Discussions

The third strategy for developing comprehension, which unfortunately is all too rare in most American classrooms, is the use of numerous deep intellectual discussions, either orally or in writing, about the meaning and significance of what the author has written. According to a growing number of scholars and practitioners, book discussions are pivotal in developing strong readers and learners. Book discussions provide opportunities for students to freely explore ideas and deepen their understanding of what they read. Research has shown that discussion not only contributes to students' comprehension of assigned texts but promotes their recall as well (Gallagher & Pearson, 1989). During discussions, students practice and refine their comprehension strategies and higher-order thinking skills, draw on their understanding of narrative and expository text organization, and develop oral language and social skills. Interactive discussions are the most effective way to develop students' speaking and listening skills and are particularly important for English language learners. Another important benefit of book discussions is that they motivate students to read, setting them on the road to becoming lifelong readers.

Planning Book Discussions

When planning discussion groups, teachers need to consider several factors—the overall purpose of the discussion, the number of participants, the type of grouping, the amount of direct instruction needed, and the roles that students will play. If the purpose is a large-group discussion of a social issue, for example, the groups should be heterogeneous to ensure that the participants will have differing opinions. Initially, students will require direct instruction in a variety of discussion skills, such as taking turns, challenging ideas rather than classmates, and supporting their positions with specific examples. Jewel and Pratt (1999) have developed a method in which teachers lead whole-class discussions, modeling how to pose good questions, find supporting evidence in the text, make connections among ideas, and elaborate on one's own ideas. After 4 to 6 weeks of these whole-class discussions, students meet in half-class discussion groups with teacher supervision for 2 to 3 weeks. Then, they try meeting in small groups on their own.

For group discussions to work, teachers cannot rely solely on students selecting books themselves. A good compromise approach is to steer students toward reading material that will have a cohesive theme or the same author by allowing them to choose from among a set of approved titles. In this way, students will still feel invested in the books they are about to read. To accommodate varying abilities, teachers should select books that represent a mix of reading levels and can include less able readers by having them listen to an audiotape of a book or read the book with a more able partner and by encouraging students to respond nonverbally to the text or in their primary language.

Ideas Behind Discussions

One point of ongoing contention is the extent to which the reader versus the aspects of the text is the source of meaning. For example, Arthur Applebee and Judith Langer have been championing reader response strategies based on in-depth discussion of students' initial responses to a particular text (see Applebee, 1992a, 1992b, 1994; Langer, 1992, 1993, 1994). What these pioneers advocate is remarkably consistent with expert recommendations in learning strategies in math and science, which are based on sophisticated teacher responses to how students are thinking about a problem.

Some advocates have taken this position too far, in part abetted by Langer's earlier writing that seemed to neglect the importance of understanding the author's message—a stance she has recently clarified. These radical constructivists claim that the content of what is read is unimportant and not very useful in educating our children because, they argue, most meaning is idiosyncratic and based in the reader's experience. That claim seems farfetched, for there are enduring childhood favorites that appeal to almost every child, and the wisdom of the past enshrined in many classics is useful knowledge that can instruct large numbers of diverse students in how to live their lives. Most children love *Charlotte's Web* and are moved by *The Diary of Anne Frank,* and every potential citizen can learn about the central principles of our democracy from *The Declaration of Independence.*

Anderson (1992), Applebee (1992a, 1992b, 1994), and Langer (1992, 1993, 1994, in press) advocate a more balanced position. They contend that there are two major types of reading comprehension—narrative or literary—in which the story is key and expository or discursive, such as the logical arguments made in science or social studies. Strategies that invoke an individual response are especially effective in deepening discussions of books. Engagement in a story often provides the vehicle for more open-ended personal responses or, in Langer's words, "exploring a horizon of possibilities" (in press, p. 37) where the interpretation of text keeps changing as deeper analysis and reader reaction interact. In addition, literary readings are one of the best vehicles for teaching students how to deal with the nuance, ambiguity, multiple perspectives, and context that have become so important in modern life.

In contrast, in comprehending writing of an expository nature, the goal is to understand the author's argument and think about the significance of that argument. Langer (in press) characterizes expository reading as "maintaining a point of reference" (p. 37)—keeping in mind the point being made and getting closer and closer to the deeper significance of that position as one reads and thinks about what has been read.

Both kinds of reading should be emphasized in schools; indeed, both kinds should be integrated in the study of literary and expository works. To use an example from high school, *Pride and Prejudice* can be the basis for expository instruction examining Jane Austen's caution about the necessity for people to learn how to look beneath the surface attractiveness of people to discern true quality and the implications of that idea for how we live our lives. Or the novel can be read for the literary engagement and self-searching that this story of a 19th-century heroine can bring to a 20th-century student (personal response).

Conversely, narrative is a powerful tool in teaching history or science; some of the best instruction asks students to argue from multiple perspectives. Commentators have accurately stressed that students are notoriously weak in the discursive—getting the point and evaluating and applying it—but unfortunately, most of our youngsters hardly ever experience nontrivial literary engagement with literature and nonfiction writing. One of the most welcome changes in some reading program materials is the balance between literary and expository works. In addition, in the past several years, there has been an explosion in the children's book market of informational titles in science, biography, history, and ethics.

In summary, according to Langer, Applebee, and other commentators, growing evidence supports the importance of exposure to exposi-

tory reading materials and writing in expository modes. Langer and Applebee warn of the twin dangers of literary instruction degenerating into countenancing the most superficial personal reactions or expository instruction becoming sterile and trivial. Some reform literature tends to downplay the significance of what Applebee (1992a, 1992b, 1994) terms the author's "message" (emphasizing the moral lesson). Proper instruction depends on balancing three literary traditions—message, reader reaction and response, and textual analysis. All of these work together to deepen understanding (Applebee, 1991).

Unfortunately, much English/language arts (ELA) instruction in elementary school neglects these strategies and settles for trivial recall questions, unmediated personal responses, and low-level follow-up activities. Many reformers warn against the mindless use of many activities that occupy the time of so many elementary students. For example, Lucy Calkins, highly respected in the ELA community, asks how doing a diorama (a craft display of an event in the book) helps develop deeper understanding. In addition, many schools and texts have underemphasized learning to understand expository text.

How to Produce More Meaningful Discussions

Discussions that delve into the deeper meanings of literary books and nonfiction should start early. Analytic comments and questions by the teacher have been shown to be major ingredients of success in effective preschool and kindergarten classes.

Leading productive discussions is a difficult art: Teachers need training both in understanding the potential issues in books children read and in the techniques of how to conduct a discussion. Several interesting projects have emerged in the process of trying to encourage deeper classroom discussions and avoiding the trivial recall or "what happened" questions that pass for comprehension discussion in most schools. Although there are differences in philosophy and the approaches fall on different parts of the child-centered/text-centered continuum, all these projects share a common strategy of deepening the response to books and engaging children in conversations about what they read.

With the Junior Great Books program, small groups (usually five to eight students) read a piece of literature selected by the students and then discuss it. The discussions are guided by a leader who asks a series of open-ended questions that help students delve deeply into the text, analyzing

the author's words and message and arriving at their own interpretations. During the initial reading, students are asked to look for and underline four things: (a) anything they do not understand or have a question about, (b) passages or words they think are especially important, (c) connections between different parts of the text, and (d) parts that elicit strong feelings or that they disagree with. One of the key rules of these discussions is that students must support their answers with evidence from the text. This reinforces both long-term memory and critical thinking skills. Students learn to listen to differing viewpoints, weigh their merits, and respond. Junior Great Books also has produced a series designed for kindergarten and first grade.

Questioning the author (QtA; Beck, McKeown, Hamilton, & Kucan, 1997) is another widely used technique. It differs from the preceding approach in that the text is selected by the teacher, typically, assigned reading in a content-area textbook. In addition, the discussion takes place during the initial reading of text and is led and managed by the teacher. The teacher poses queries that stimulate and focus discussion to help students grapple with each portion of text. Although the QtA procedures differ from other book discussion techniques, they all have the same goal: having students work together, actively engaged in and responsible for constructing meaning.

In the literature circle approach (Short & Klassen, 1993), students meet in self-selected groups after reading preassigned segments of a text. Discussions are led by the students, using response logs to launch discussion. The teacher may be present to act as both knowledgeable reader and mentor (Samway & Whang, 1996). After each meeting, students use checklists to evaluate their participation. Teachers can extend students' learning by asking them to complete writing assignments further exploring certain issues or literary elements and then arranging follow-up discussion groups. The reading workshop (Atwell, 1987) is another method for encouraging a personal response to reading. It begins with a teacher-led, whole-class minilesson. The primary focus is silent, self-selected reading and response in the form of journal writing, teacher conferencing, or small group discussion. Each workshop ends with a sharing time.

Richard Anderson's (1995) "Learning to Argue" strategy is aimed at the discourse side of literature. Students read a story about an immigrant Chinese American boy and discuss whether or not the boy's desire to change his name is a good thing or a bad thing to do. They learn to marshal arguments and justify positions. Taffy Raphael and Susan McMahon have instituted a successful book club program with local schools in Mich-

igan (Raphael, 1994; see also Goatley, Brock, & Raphael, 1995; Raphael & Goatley, 1994; Raphael, Goatley, McMahon, & Woodman, 1995). The Reading for Real Program (ages 4 to 8) from Eric Schaps's Developmental Studies Center in Oakland, California, takes favorites of children's literature and helps teachers think about the possibilities for discussion. St. John's College in Annapolis, Maryland, has produced the Touchstones Discussion Project. Last, several of the best writing projects around the nation have now become involved in combining writing processes around deeper issues in literature and public discourse. Bob Calfee from Stanford University's Project READ has stressed critical literacy (Calfee & Patrick, 1995). Many of these projects use reading logs or follow-up activities as strategies.

Assessment

As explained in previous chapters, to reach the long-term goals of fluency and comprehension, students need to master a number of precursor foundation skills. Assessment in the early grades, therefore, needs to be frequent and specific to gauge students' progress in achieving critical benchmarks. (See *CORE Assessing Reading* for tests of phonological awareness and decoding and word attack skills.) If these benchmarks are not met, intervention is indicated. The following chart recaps the important literacy benchmarks for kindergarten through second grade.

Grade Level	Assessed Skill	Benchmark
Kindergarten (midyear)	Print concepts & alphabet recognition	Can identify parts of a book
		Knows most letter names and shapes (upper- and lowercase)
	Phonemic awareness	Can identify the first sound in words
Kindergarten (end)	Print concepts & alphabet recognition	Can use basic print conventions to track text—word boundaries and left-to-right sweeps
		Knows all letter names and shapes
	Phonemic awareness	Can identify the first and last sounds in words

Grade Level	Assessed Skill	Benchmark
		Can orally blend segmented CVC words
	Decoding	Grasps the alphabetic principle
		Knows some letter/sound correspondences—all single consonants and short vowels
		Knows some sight words
	Listening comprehension	Can retell a familiar story
Grade 1 (midyear)	Print concepts & alphabet recognition	Full print awareness—can identify titles and authors
	Phonemic awareness	Can identify the first, last, and medial sounds in words
	Decoding	Can decode real and nonsense CVC words (including consonant digraphs), words with consonant blends, and words with the long-vowel pattern VCe
		Can automatically recognize 50 out of 300 high-frequency words
		Can read simple multisyllabic words using basic word attack strategies—breaking compound words into two known words and identifying common endings, such as -ed and -ing
	Listening comprehension	Can retell main ideas of narratives
Grade 1 (end)	Decoding	Can decode words with more complex patterns—high-utility vowel digraphs, r-controlled vowels, variant vowels, diphthongs, double consonants, silent consonants

Grade Level	Assessed Skill	Benchmark
		Can automatically recognize 150 high-frequency words
		Can read multisyllabic words using VC/CV syllabication
	Reading fluency	Can read aloud with natural expression at a rate of 60 words correct per minute
Grade 2	Reading comprehension	Can identify story elements
		Can retell main ideas of simple expository or narrative text
	Decoding	(Learns remaining basic phonics patterns through direct teaching and independent reading)
		Can automatically recognize all 300 high-frequency words
		Can decode real and nonsense multisyllabic words using knowledge of syllable types, common division patterns, and morphemic units

In upper grades, there are a variety of measures to identify students who are struggling with reading. The challenge facing educators is to determine why particular students are being held back and to plan appropriate intervention. As explained in Chapter 5, in contrast to the discrete skills measurement in the lower grades, assessment in the upper grades generally begins with the global skills of comprehension and reading fluency. (See CORE Assessing Reading for tests of these skills.) Tests of reading comprehension use multiple-choice questions, open-ended questions, or cloze passage techniques to measure students' understanding of passages and whole text. In these tests, students draw on their word recognition skills, their syntactic knowledge, and their strategic reading and high-order reasoning skills. This broad-based testing is the starting point for planning instruction and grouping in the upper grades. As explained previously, if students show poor comprehension on these initial assessments, follow-up fluency and decoding diagnostic assessments should be used to pinpoint the particular subskills that are causing reading difficulty. The *CORE Teaching Reading Sourcebook* has detailed instructions for curriculum-based measurement of oral reading fluency using the ORF norms developed by Hasbrouck and Tindal (1992). The midyear target rates for third through fifth grades are as follows: Grade 3: about 93 WCPM; Grade 4: about 112 WCPM; Grade 5: about 118 WCPM.

Because spelling knowledge supports fluent reading and writing, it is also important to monitor students' spelling development throughout the grades. Spelling inventories help teachers examine students' spelling errors and plan instruction based on their level of understanding of the sound and structure of words (Bear et al., 2000; See *CORE Assessing Reading* for elementary and upper level spelling inventories.) Vocabulary also warrants assessment because it is so closely tied to comprehension. The *Critchlow Verbal Language Scales* in *CORE Assessing Reading* assess oral vocabulary, which in turn support reading vocabulary.

In addition to specific reading assessments, ongoing assessment is necessary to monitor students' progress and further define the focus of instruction. Teacher observations, curriculum tasks, and reading conferences provide opportunities to monitor students' independent reading and to assess their syntactic awareness, vocabulary and concept development, and strategic reading skills.

8

Writing and Speaking

Written and Oral Applications

In the context of teaching reading, writing and speaking play important roles. As explained previously, dictation activities connect the encoding process (writing) to the decoding process (reading) by demonstrating that the same sound/spelling knowledge students use to read enables them to communicate with others through writing. Regular dictation of words containing patterns taught in phonics lessons and previously taught high-frequency words reinforces students' learning, develops their auditory skills, and offers teachers valuable insight into their progress.

Speaking and listening skills are also key elements of most ELA programs. Previous chapters have dealt with the importance of these skills in developing fluency, vocabulary knowledge, and comprehension. Throughout the grades, students should listen to text read aloud and take part in rich discussions about books, ideas, and important matters. The more that students participate in these deep discussions, the more significant the increases in listening comprehension, which in turn enhance reading comprehension (Juel, 1994). Beginning in preschool and kindergarten, students should be asked to orally retell stories, repeat nursery rhymes and songs, tell a story, and discuss both literature and nonfiction. From first grade, students should be able to describe an event or setting and provide explanations of characters' motives. Starting in second grade, students should refine their listening and speaking skills by learning to take turns and respond to others in discussion groups and by performing in plays and Readers Theater. The goal is for students to become proficient in the major types of oral activities that occur in school and in the real world:

- Organizing materials to present an oral report
- Making a persuasive argument
- Recommending a course of action
- Conveying information
- Fully participating in group discussions

Writing

Some of the best writing curricula have been devised by teachers in various writing projects around the country. Many of these projects have been in existence for several years and have helped thousands of teachers learn how to write and how to teach the process of writing. One of the central principles of this movement is that understanding is created by writing. They argue that until students write about something, their views are inchoate. Thus, keeping journals, free-writing techniques, multiple drafts, peer review, postponing editing until the final draft, and other techniques have emerged as ways to assist students to think through and organize their ideas before they write and then to rethink and revise their initial drafts. The aim of these techniques is to encourage students to think about what they are writing and in the process, to refine, reformulate, and extend their understanding of a subject.

Although the process approach has now become the conventional wisdom among ELA professionals, some cautionary notes have been being raised about overreliance on this strategy. According to Arthur Applebee (1986, 1991, p. 401), who has also been one of the most respected commentators on the course of writing instruction in the past decade, the process approach arose as a response to the perceived ineffectiveness of the traditional composition classes in high school. Composition classes tended to emphasize correct usage and mechanics, the use of topic sentences, and formulas for paragraph construction. This instruction relied on sampling traditional modes of discourse and analyzing classic examples of good form in different discourses, such as narration or exposition, learning the rules that govern those examples, and practicing following those rules.

The process approach grew out of research showing that writing, rather than being a linear process, involves a number of "recursively operating subprocesses (for example, planning, monitoring, drafting, revision, editing)" (Applebee, 1986, p. 96), and that expert and novice writers differ in their use of those subprocesses. Thus, teach the processes.

One major problem with this strategy is that another important finding of what constitutes good writing—tailoring the use of processes to the nature of the task—was ignored. Much writing instruction in the process approach has become formulaic: It encourages students to go through the techniques, regardless of the nature of the task and detached from writing for a real purpose. The processes have become the end instead of the means.

Just as students need to be exposed to a wide range of reading materials, they need to develop their skill with different writing modes. Although 50% of all writing in high school occurs outside of the English class (Applebee, 1986), writing instruction has been focused primarily on personal and imaginative writing. This type of writing has little relevance in science and history classes where the purpose of much of the writing is review and reinforcement, not extension or refinement. In these classes, assignments are typically a page or less, first and final drafts are completed within a day, and the assignments serve to examine students in a given subject matter. Process writing is overkill in these situations.

Thus there is a potential disjuncture between writing instruction in English classes and the writing occurring outside those classes. Obviously, part of the problem is that not enough activities requiring reasoning and problem solving are being assigned. But a major deficiency in writing instruction is that the strategic purpose for writing has been misconceptualized by too many.

Applebee (1986) posits three major purposes of writing. These are to

1. Draw on relevant experience and knowledge in preparation for new activities
2. Consolidate and review new information and experiences
3. Reformulate and extend knowledge

Process writing instruction should be about figuring out which processes apply in which situation. Creative writing, which has become the mainstay of many elementary writing programs, applies only to a portion of the third purpose.

Another major problem with overreliance on a process approach is that content tends to become trivialized. The *how* of writing is not enough. *What* students think and write about is key to developing literacy skills. Process learning must be combined with deep understanding of literature.

Last, there has been an unfortunate reluctance on the part of many teachers to insist on a polished final draft. In reaction to student deficiencies in these areas, many writing projects are now attempting to put more emphasis on the correctness of the final product by insisting on proper spelling, punctuation, grammar, and mechanics without losing the benefits of students putting their ideas on paper. Still other projects are also putting more emphasis on expository writing and public discourse to remedy the overreliance on narrative and expressive writing.

9

Frequently Asked Questions

How should English language learners be taught to read?

For teachers, students, and their families, the results of many past bilingual programs have been disappointing. Often in these programs, the English literacy component was weak, and many students failed even to become proficient readers in their primary languages. Whether second-language learners are in regular classrooms or bilingual classrooms, the same principles outlined in this book for learning to read in English apply. All students need systematic, explicit instruction in an organized, comprehensive English reading program. In addition, a strong English language development program beginning in kindergarten and first grade is crucial. In the past, many people felt that reading instruction in English had to be delayed until students had more fully developed their English oral language skills. However, there is now wide agreement that the old model of delaying transition to English reading until third or fourth grade makes it extremely unlikely that English language learners will ever catch up to their English-speaking peers. Moreover, recent research and best practices have shown that young English language learners can learn to read in English with the same results as peers whose primary language is English (Morgan & Willows, 1998).

Bernhardt and Kamil (1998) have examined the special challenges faced by children who are learning to read in a second language. They offer teachers the cardinal rule, "remember everything you know about first-language reading when you are teaching reading to speakers of other languages" and propose the following instructional guidelines:

- Recognize students' strengths, and teach more content, not less.
- Demand critical thinking and the type of deep understanding of text that the QtA method encourages.
- Provide instruction in the basic skills and strategies that all students need to master to become proficient readers.
- Use informational texts as an integral part of instruction.
- Create an "I-can-do-it!" attitude, and encourage students to challenge the racism and classism that are often directed toward non-native speakers of English.

Because the overlap between languages can be as much as 20%, teachers do not have to start at the very beginning with students who are literate in their first language (Bernhardt & Kamil, 1995). Rather, they can focus on the particular language features—phonology, orthography, morphology, syntax, tense, and lexicon—that are different in the student's primary language than in English. Bernhardt and Kamil's research also indicates that at least 30% of the process of second-language reading involves grammatical and lexical knowledge. The more English words students know and the more English sentence structures they learn, the better off they will be.

In response to recent research, some ESL and ELD programs now use grade-level content as the vehicle for language development. This ensures that every student has access to the core curriculum while learning the vocabulary and concepts, academic language, and critical thinking skills they will need to succeed in their school careers.

Can learning formal phonics rules help students learn to read?

Some people think phonics can be taught by spending considerable time on learning formal phonics rules on pronunciation of vowels (e.g., "In many two- and three-syllable words, the final *e* makes the preceding vowel long"), pronunciation of consonants, division of syllables, and accentuation of syllables. Not so, says Adams (1990, p. 272). First, it would take an enormous effort to memorize the approximately 121 rules.

Moreover, in examining the most common 45 generalizations, researchers found an extremely low reliability rate, whereas the ones that did conform to the rules reliably were used infrequently. Many of the common ones were riddled with exceptions. For example, the rule just cited about lengthening vowels turns out to be true only 46% of the time.

Many generalizations use technical terms, such as *consonant* and *short vowel*, that are not really understood by many young children.

Another problem with learning to read by learning the rules is that most people find trying to apply an abstract rule to an immediate situation to be a very inefficient way of operating. Rules have to be consciously applied and can never substitute for speed of direct familiarity with the patterns to which they apply. (Think of trying to apply the grammar rules learned in taking a foreign language or even stopping to translate thoughts from English to Spanish in trying to speak or understand that language. The process must become unconscious and automatic to be effective.) Adams (1990) warns that "for neither the expert nor the novice can rote knowledge of an abstract rule, in and of itself, make any difference" (p. 272). Nevertheless, Adams suggests that the use of some phonics rules is helpful in learning the patterns. Their use must be supplemental and resorted to only after the recognition system fails. They are helpful in getting students to attend to the pattern relationships in a word and can be used to overcome particular stumbling blocks with dyslexic children.

10

Conclusions

In the past decade, those interested in improving schools have invested huge amounts of time and money in a variety of complex strategies, including standards-based education, comprehensive school reform networks, restructuring, charter schools, and accountability schemes. In the past few years, another more straightforward strategy has been gaining credibility: get the basics of literacy right by investing in professional training that is grounded in proven research, purchasing top-flight materials, and giving reading the highest administrative priority. This approach is not only lower in cost and more efficient but produces better results in student performance in reading and in other subjects areas. The former strategies can also incorporate direct literacy improvement as a crucial component.

With such massive support for the convergent findings of research, there really is no excuse for not adopting these ideas in every classroom and school in this country. Yet millions of students continue to suffer from preventable reading difficulties because of the lack of effective reading instruction. We owe it to these students and their families to apply the powerful knowledge delineated in this book in every classroom, school, and district in this country. The school community should not accept anything less.

Resource A

Table A.1 Common Consonant Sound/Spellings

Phoneme	Spelling (Initial Position)	Key Word	Spelling (Final Position)	Key Word
/b/	b	bat	b	tub
/d/	d	day	d	bad
/f/	f	fat	f	leaf
	ph	phone	ff	off
			ph	graph
			gh	laugh
/g/	g	get	g	big
	gu	guitar	gue	plague
	gh	ghost	gg	egg
/h/	h	how		
	wh	who		
/j/	j	jump	ge	cage
	g	giant	dge	ledge
/k/	c	cat	k	lock
	k	kite	ck	clock
	ch	choir		
/l/	l	let	ll	well
/m/	m	mat	m	swam
			mb	lamb
			mn	hymn
/n/	n	net	n	man
	kn	knock	gn	sign
	gn	gnat		
/p/	p	pet	p	top

Table A.1   Continued

Phoneme	Spelling (Initial Position)	Key Word	Spelling (Final Position)	Key Word
/r/	r	rat	r	far
	wr	write		
/s/	s	sat	ce	race
	c	city	se	vase
	ps	psychology	ss	kiss
			s	bus
/t/	t	top	t	sit
			bt	doubt
			ed	skipped
/v/	v	vine	ve	love
/w/	w	wave		
/y/	y	yellow		
/z/	z	zoo	se	these
			ze	freeze
			zz	buzz
			s	has
			z	whiz
/ch/	ch	chin	ch	beach
			tch	match
/sh/	sh	shoe	sh	wish
	s	sugar		
/zh/	si (medial position)	vision		
	s (medial position)	pleasure		
	z (medial position)	azure		
/th/	th	thank	th	path
/TH/	th	this	the	bathe
/hw/	wh	what		
/ng/			ng	sing

SOURCE: Honig et al. (2000). Reprinted by permission.

Table A.2 Common Vowel Sound/Spellings

Sound									
/ā/	a_e (made)	ai (wait)	ay (day)	ea (great)	ei (veil)	ey (they)	eigh (sleigh)		
/ē/	e (me)	ee (feet)	ea (bead)	y (many)	ie (field)	e_e (these)	ey (key)	i_e (machine)	ei (receive)
/ī/	i_e (time)	y (sky)	i (kind)	ie (pie)	igh (high)	ye (dye)			
/ō/	o (so)	o_e (hope)	oa (coat)	ow (low)	oe (toe)	ou (soul)	ew (sew)		
/a/	a (sat)	a_e (have)							
/e/	e (pet)	ea (head)	ai (said)	a (many)					
/i/	i (six)	y (gym)	e (pretty)	i_e (give)	ee (been)	ui (build)			
/o/	o (log)	a (watch)							
/u/	u (but)	o (ton)	o_e (love)	ou (young)					
/ə/	a (above)	e (system)	i (easily)	o (gallop)	u (circus)				
/ûr/	ur (turn)	ir (bird)	er (her)	or (work)					
/är/	ar (car)								
/ôr/	or (or)	our (pour)	ar (war)						
/aw/	aw (saw)	au (cause)	a[l] (walk)	a[ll] (tall)	ou (cough)	au (taught)			
/oi/ /oy/	oi (soil)	oy (boy)							
/ou/ /ow/	ou (cloud)	ow (now)							
/oo/ (yoo)a	oo (hoot)	u (July)	ue (blue)	ew (new)	u_e (tube)	o (do)	ou (soup)		
/o͝o/	oo (book)	u (put)	o (wolf)	ou (would)					

SOURCE: Honig et al. (2000). Reprinted by permission.
a. As in *cube* and *fuel*.

Table A.3 Sound/Spelling Percentages

CONSONANTS

/b/	b (97%), bb	/w/	w (92%)
/d/	d (98%), dd, ed	/y/	y (44%), i (55%)
/f/	f (78%), ff, ph, lf	/z/	z (23%), zz, s (64%)
/g/	g (88%), gg, gh	/ch/	ch (55%), t (31%)
/h/	h (98%), wh	/sh/	sh (26%), ti (53%), ssi, s, si, sci
/j/	g (66%), j (22%), dg	/zh/	si (49%), s (33%), ss, z
/k/	c (73%), cc, k (13%), ck, lk, q	/th/	th (100%)
/l/	l (91%), ll	/TH/	th (100%)
/m/	m (94%), mm	/hw/	wh (100%)
/n/	n (97%), mm, kn, gn	/ng/	n (41%), ng (59%)
/p/	p (96%), pp		
/r/	r (97%), rr, wr		VOWELS
/s/	s (73%), c (17%), ss	/ā/	a (45%), a_e (35%), ai, ay, ea
/t/	t (97%), tt, ed	/ē/	e (70%), ea (10%), ee (10%), ie, e, e_e, ey, i, ei y
/v/	v (99.5%), f (of)	/ī/	i_e (37%), i (37%), y (14%), ie, y_e, igh

132

Phoneme	Spellings
/ō/	o (73%), o_e (14%), ow, oa, oe
/a/	a (97%)
/e/	e (91%), ea, e_e (15%)
/i/	i (68%), y (23%)
/o/	o (79%)
/u/	u (86%), o, ou
/ə/	a (24%), e (13%), i (22%), o (27%), u
/ûr/	er (40%), ir (13%), ur (26%)

Phoneme	Spellings
/är/	ar (89%)
/ôr/	or (41%)
/aw/	o, a, au, aw, ough, augh
/oi/	oi (62%), oy (29%)
/ou/	ou (56%), ow (29%)
/o͞o/	oo (38%), u (21%), o,ou, u_e, ew, ue
/yo͞o/	u (69%), u_e (22%), ew, ue
/o͝o/	oo (31%), u (54%), ou, o (8%), ould

Resource B

The Role of Skills in a Comprehensive Elementary Reading Program—24 Major Points

 The goal of any early reading program should be to enable almost every student to

- Read fluently and understand grade-appropriate material by the end of elementary school
- Read a large number of books, magazines, and informational text
- Reach high levels of comprehension ability
- Enjoy and be able to learn from reading

For most students, this goal can be accomplished only if they can decode and are able to read beginning books by mid-first grade.

Why a Skills Strand Is an Essential Part of a Comprehensive Reading Program

All Children Need Skills Support

1. Language- and literature-rich classrooms are essential for effective reading programs, but almost all children need some organized skills instruction to reach optimal levels. For some groups of children, the consequences of the absence of an explicit, organized skills strand are especially severe. Up to 40% of these students will remain, in effect, nonreaders, and significantly more than half will not read proficiently.

What Proficient Readers Do

2. Proficient readers recognize words automatically from their letter patterns, aided by the meaning and context of what is being read.

How Students Become Fluent Readers

3. Proficient readers become automatic by recognizing a specific word *successfully* numerous times (in the range of 4 to 15 times during the early stages of reading). Encountering the word in the context of reading for meaning reduces the number of successful attempts necessary.

4. The most effective way for children to become fluent with a specific word is for them to consciously process both the letter patterns and sounds of the word the first few times it is read. For beginning readers, a combination of repeated reading of familiar material and tackling new material builds a critical mass of automatically recognized words, which in turn multiplies the number of books or materials a student can read.

Why Students Need to Successfully Read
Large Amounts of Material Early On

5. The pathway to reading fluency (recognizing 90% to 95% of the words for grade-appropriate material) is to read a substantial amount of text each year, beginning at least by the middle of first grade. At the early grades, most stories or informational text will contain significant numbers of words important to the story that are already in the student's oral vocabulary but are not yet automatically recognizable in print. If students are to successfully read these materials, they must be able to decode new words. Until students have mastered the basic letter/sound patterns and a set of high-frequency words, text should be designed to ensure that most words follow the specific patterns and high-frequency words that have been previously taught—decodable text—to avoid confusion about the complex English letter/sound system.

Becoming Readers by Mid-First Grade

Establishing Goals

6. If a school, district, or state wants to maximize reading performance for all students, it should establish a goal that as many students as
possible will become readers by mid-first grade. Only by achieving this
measure of independent reading of beginning materials will students
encounter sufficient text early enough to become proficient. Only 1 out
of 8 students who cannot read grade-appropriate materials at the end of
first grade will ever catch up without extraordinary intervention strategies.

Benchmarks and Instruction:
Kindergarten and Early First Grade

7. To become readers by mid-first grade, the following must occur:
* Students must leave *kindergarten* knowing letter names, shapes,
  and some letter sounds; possessing basic phonemic, syntactic, and
  print awareness; and having listening, discussion, and oral telling
  and retelling skills.
* During the first 4 months of first grade, they must learn basic
  sound/symbol system correspondences, more advanced phonemic
  and syntactic awareness, blending and word-attack strategic skills,
  automatic recognition of basic high-frequency words and word
  families, comprehension skills, and how to use these tools in combination to read for meaning. Writing out and spelling out words
  (especially those they are reading), which necessitates encoding
  sounds into letter patterns, is also one of the best ways to learn
  phonics.

The Relationship of Word Recognition,
Decoding, and Phonemic Awareness

8. The most important component of reading ability in first grade is
word recognition, the most important component of word recognition is
decoding ability, and the most important components of decoding ability
are phonemic awareness (the ability to hear and consciously manipulate

the sounds in words) and phonics (knowing the system of letter/letter pattern/sound correspondences and how to use that system in decoding words).

The Importance of Phonemic Awareness

9. An estimated 1 out of 5 children cannot learn decoding because they cannot hear or consciously manipulate the sounds in words. Almost every poor reader and more than 50% of special education youngsters lack this proficiency in phonemic awareness; it cannot be overcome without instruction.

10. Fortunately for the children who lack phonemic awareness, about 14 hours of specially designed kindergarten instruction (rhyming and word play), in addition to their regular instruction, will provide the necessary foundation to learn decoding in the first grade.

Instruction: First Grade (January to June)

11. After the December or January milestone, students should read a large number (100 to 200) of beginning narrative and informational texts as the primary learning strategy to become automatic with increasing numbers of words. Teachers need to monitor progress.

Instruction: Mid-First Grade On

Developing Vocabulary and Being Well-Read

12. Starting in late first grade, students should read about 25 to 35 age-appropriate fiction and informational books a year if they are to be grade-level readers by the end of elementary school. Students need to learn about 3,000 to 4,000 new vocabulary words (words not yet in their speaking vocabulary) each year (or about 70 words per week) during the elementary (and secondary) grades to be able to read and understand grade-appropriate material. In addition, each school needs to implement a vocabulary development program with explicit instruction aimed at

helping students learn new words more efficiently during reading, teaching specific meanings of selected words, and listening to rich language.

Specific Comprehension Strategies

13. After initial basic comprehension instruction in how to read for meaning in first grade (supplemented by similar instruction about the stories read to or shown to children), an organized comprehension strand should be initiated that includes three components: independent reading, strategic reading, and book clubs or discussion of materials read in common, using a wide range of fiction and nonfiction materials to engender deep discussions about what has been read. All students should be able to read and understand a variety of grade-level materials as well as reach the higher comprehension levels of inferring, connecting, and applying what they have read.

Instruction in More Advanced Decoding, Complex Phonics, Syllabication, Vocabulary, and Mechanics Skills

14. Skills instruction in more complex decoding strategies should continue after the beginning independent reading stage is reached in the more advanced areas of symbol/sound relationships, syllabication, morphemic analysis, spelling and mechanics, grammar, word roots and affixes, and vocabulary.

Writing

15. Students should have an organized writing program. Writing should prepare students to tell a story, organize a report, argue a point, and explain a phenomenon according to acceptable rubrics.

Temporary Spelling

16. In kindergarten and early first grade, temporary or invented spellings (approximations) are appropriate to help children write and learn about the connection of sounds to letters. However, starting in mid-

dle to later first grade, incorrect spellings should be corrected in final draft so that erroneous patterns are not reinforced and to convey the important message that spelling matters. Invented spelling is an extremely effective diagnostic tool throughout the grades to assist teachers in determining how well a student is learning phonics and the underlying structure of English orthography.

Spelling

17. Students should have an organized spelling program from late first grade on. Learning to spell helps students learn to read. Spelling activities should be connected to the words students are reading and writing, should systematically introduce them to orthographic patterns, and should ensure that they learn spelling demons. Each week, students should learn 20 words; approximately half will be words they cannot yet spell. Word lists should be tailored to each individual student's stage of spelling development. Instruction should incorporate the pretest-study-posttest method to ensure students study only words they do not know, self-correcting of student tests, proofreading activities, and strategies for remembering spelling patterns. Students should practice using these words in writing.

Implications for Instruction

Flexibility

18. Most students will be able to meet the mid-first-grade timetable for independent reading of beginning material. Some will reach this level earlier. Some will take longer. Some will need intensified instruction (for example, more time with the teacher) to meet this timetable. Classrooms and schools should be able to accommodate these differences while bringing most children to this level by the mid-first-grade benchmark. When students can read beginning material independently, teachers must ensure that most of the material students read is in the 90% to 95% recognition range.

Dynamic, Not Rote, Teaching

19. Phonemic awareness, phonics, and decoding should be taught in a dynamic, thinking manner so that students come to understand the alphabetic principle and the system of symbol/sound correspondences and how to consciously figure out new words. Programs should provide materials and activities that give students enough practice so that the particular skill being taught becomes second nature. Programs also should provide opportunities to develop and use these skills by having students read text with and without the teacher. A disconnected, worksheet-driven phonics program will not be effective.

Sufficient Time

20. In kindergarten, at least one third of the day should be devoted to language arts activities. In early primary grades, students should spend at least 2 to 3 hours in language arts activities, including reading and writing in the other subjects. At least 60 to 90 minutes of this time should be concentrated on reading and activities, including guided, shared, and independent reading; student conferencing; the skills strands; and word play.

Availability of Reading Material

21. Reading material must be available so that students are continually reading at about the 95% recognition level (1 new word out of 20). If books are too easy, no growth occurs; if they are too hard, students become frustrated and will not become automatic with enough words. Teachers should ensure that books are appropriate to students' reading levels by continually conferencing with them. Students should read 25 to 35 books a year after first grade. Narrative, informational, and magazine text should be available.

Role of Parents

22. Parents should be enlisted to support the development of their child's reading skills by reading to their child, listening to their child read, and discussing what has been read.

Intervention for Students Who Are Falling Behind

23. If more intense instruction does not allow a student to meet reading milestones, tutors should be made available for those students not learning reading skills early. A back-up program of basic skills should be in place for students who transfer in at second grade or beyond or who need reinforcement.

Spanish-Speaking Children in Bilingual Programs

24. English language learners can be successfully taught to read in English in much the same way as students whose primary language is English.

Spanish-speaking students who are in bilingual classes should be able to reach the code-breaking or reading stage in their primary language a few months earlier (many of them by the end of kindergarten) because Spanish is phonetically regular and composed of highly regular syllables. Bilingual programs should provide a comprehensive English language development component in first grade that will help students understand the English sound/symbol patterns, syllables, and morphology and enable them to do extensive reading in English.

References

Adams, M. J. (1990). *Beginning to read: Thinking and learning about print.* Cambridge, MA: MIT Press.

Adams, M. J. (1991). Why not phonics *and* whole language? In *All language and the creation of literacy* (pp. 40-53). *Proceedings of the Orton Dyslexia Society Symposia, "Whole Language and Phonics" and "Literacy and Language."* Baltimore: Orton Dyslexia Society.

Adams, M. J., & Bruck, M. (1995). Resolving the "Great Debate." *American Educator, 19*(7), 10-20.

Adams, M. J., Foorman, B. R., Lundberg, I., & Beeler, T. (1998). *Phonemic awareness in young children.* Baltimore: Paul H. Brookes.

Allington, R. L. (1983). Fluency: The neglected goal. *The Reading Teacher, 36,* 556-561.

Allington, R. L. (1991). Children who find learning to read difficult: School responses to diversity. In E. H. Hiebert (Ed.), *Literacy for a diverse society* (pp. 237-252). New York: Teachers College Press.

Anderson, R. C. (1992). *Research foundations for wide reading* (paper commissioned by the World Bank). Urbana, IL: Center for the Study of Reading.

Anderson, R. C. (1995, April). *Children's argumentation during story discussions.* Invited address at the annual meeting of the American Educational Research Association, San Francisco.

Anderson, R. C., & Freebody, P. (1981). Vocabulary knowledge. In J. Guthrie (Ed.), *Comprehension and teaching research reviews* (pp. 77-117). Newark, DE: International Reading Association.

Anderson, R. C., Hiebert, E. H., Scott, J. A., & Wilkinson, I. A. G. (1985). *Becoming a nation of readers: The report of the Commission on Reading.* Champaign, IL: Center for the Study of Reading and National Academy of Education.

Anderson. R. C., & Nagy, W. E. (1991). Word meaning. In R. Barr, M. L. Kamil, P. B. Mosenthal, & P. D. Pearson (Eds.), *Handbook of reading research* (Vol. 2, pp. 690-724). White Plains, NY: Longman.

Anderson, R. C., & Nagy, W. E. (1992). The vocabulary conundrum. *American Educator, 17,* 14-18, 44-49.

Anderson, R. C., & Pearson, P. D. (1984). A schema-theoretic view of basic processes in reading comprehension. In P. D. Pearson, R. Barr, M. L. Kamil, P. B. Mosenthal, & P. D. Pearson (Eds.), *Handbook of reading research* (Vol. 1). White Plains, NY: Longman.

Anderson, R.C., Wilson, P. T., & Fielding, L. G. (1988). Growth in reading and how children spend their time outside of school. *Reading Research Quarterly, 23*(3), 285-303.

Applebee, A. N. (1986). Problems in process approaches: Toward a reconceptualization of process instruction. In A. R. Petrosky & D. Bartholomae (Eds.). *The teaching of writing: Eighty-fifth year book of the National Society for the Study of Education* (pp. 95-113). Chicago: University of Chicago Press.

Applebee, A. N. (1991). Informal reasoning and writing instruction. In J. E. Voss, D. N. Perkins, & J. W. Segal (Eds.), *Informal reasoning and education* (pp. 401-414). Hillsdale, NJ: Lawrence Erlbaum.

Applebee, A. N. (1992a). The background for reform: Rethinking literature instruction. In J. A. Langer (Ed.), *Literature instruction: A focus on student response* (pp. 1-17). Urbana, IL: National Council of Teachers of English.

Applebee, A. N. (1992b). Stability and change in the high school canon. *English Journal, 81*(5), 27-32.

Applebee, A. N. (1994). Toward thoughtful curriculum: Fostering discipline-based conversation. *English Journal, 83*(2), 45-52.

Atwell, N. (1987). *In the middle: Writing, reading, and learning with adolescents.* Portsmouth, NH: Heinemann.

Ball, E. W., & Blachman, A. (1991). Does phoneme awareness training in kindergarten make a difference in early word recognition and developmental spelling? *Reading Research Quarterly, 26,* 33-44.

Baumann, J. F., & Kameenui, E. J. (1991). Research on vocabulary instruction: Ode to Voltaire. In J. Flood, D. Lapp, & J. R. Squire (Eds.), *Handbook of research on teaching the English language arts* (pp. 604-632). New York: Macmillan.

Bear, D. (1991). *Determining criteria for the development of a qualitative scale of higher levels of orthographic knowledge.* Unpublished study. University of Nevada-Reno, Reno.

Bear, D., Invernizzi, M., Templeton, S., & Johnston, F. (2000). *Words their way: Word study for phonics, vocabulary, and spelling instruction.* Upper Saddle River, NJ: Prentice Hall.

Beck, I., & Juel, C. (1995). The role of decoding in learning to read. *American Educator, 19*(8), 21-25, 39-42.

Beck, I. L., McKeown, M. G., Hamilton, R. L., & Kucan, L. (1997). *Questioning the author: An approach for enhancing student engagement with text.* Newark, DE: International Reading Association.

Beers, J., Cramer, R., & Hammond, D. (1995). *Spelling: An overview of research and current research information and practices.* Glenview, IL: Scott Foresman.

Bernhardt, E. B. (1991). *Reading development in a second language.* Norwood, NJ: Ablex.

Bernhardt, E. B., & Kamil, M. (1995). Interpreting relationships between L1 and L2 reading: Consolidating the linguistic threshold and the linguistic interdependence hypotheses. *Applied Linguistics, 16,* 15-34.

Bernhardt, E. B., & Kamil, M. (1998). Literacy instruction for non-native speakers of English. In M. F. Graves, C. Juel, & B. B. Graves (Eds.), *Teaching reading in the twenty-first century* (pp. 432-475). Needham Heights, MA: Allyn & Bacon.

Berninger, V. (1997). Educational and biological links to learning disabilities. *Perspectives, 23.*

Biemiller, A. (1994). Some observations on beginning reading instruction. *Educational Psychologist, 29,* 203-209.

Blachman, B. A. (1991). Getting ready to read: Learning how print maps to speech. In J. Kavanagh (Ed.), *The language continuum: From infancy to literacy* (pp. 1-22, reprinted.). Washington, DC: U.S. Department of Health and Human Services.

Blachowicz, C., & Fisher, P. (1996). *Teaching vocabulary in all classrooms.* Upper Saddle River, NJ: Prentice Hall.

Blevins, W. (1998). *Phonics from A to Z: A practical guide.* New York: Scholastic.

Brown, A. L., & Palincsar, A. S. (1984). Reciprocal teaching of comprehension fostering and comprehension monitoring. *Cognition and Instruction, 1,* 117-175.

Brown, H., & Cambourne, B. (1987). *Read and retell: A strategy for the whole-language/natural learning classroom.* Portsmouth, NH: Heinemann.

Bruck, M., & Treiman, R. (1990). Phonological awareness and spelling in normal children and dyslexics: The case of initial consonant clusters. *Journal of Experimental Child Psychology, 50.*

Bryson, B. (1990). *The mother tongue: English & how it got that way.* New York: William Morrow.

Calfee, R. C., & Patrick, C. L. (1995). *Teach our children well: Bringing K-12 education into the 21st century.* Stanford, CA: Stanford Alumni Association.

California Department of Education. (1994). *I can learn: A handbook for parents, teachers, and students.* Sacramento: Author.

California State Board of Education. (1999). *Reading/language arts framework for California public schools: Kindergarten through grade twelve.* Sacramento: California Department of Education.

Carnine, D. W., Silbert, J., & Kameenui, E. J. (1997). *Direct instruction reading* (3rd ed.). Upper Saddle River, NJ: Prentice Hall.

Carr, E., & Ogle, D. (1987). K-W-L Plus: A strategy for comprehension and summarization. *Journal of Reading 30,* 626-636.

Carver, R. P., & Leibert, R. (1995). The effect of reading library books at different levels of difficulty upon gain in reading ability. *Reading Research Quarterly, 30,* 26-50.

Center for the Study of Reading. (n.d.). *Teachers and independent reading.* Champaign, IL: University of Illinois at Urbana-Champaign. Reading Research and Education Center.

Chall, J. S. (1983). *Learning to read: The great debate.* New York: McGraw-Hill.

Chall, J. S. (1987). Two vocabularies for reading: Recognition and meaning. In M. G. McKeown & M. E. Curtis (Eds.), *The nature of vocabulary acquisition* (pp. 7-18). Mahwah, NJ: Erlbaum.

Chall, J. S. (1989). Learning to read: The great debate 20 years later. *Phi Delta Kappan, 70*, 521-538.

Chall, J. S. (1992). The new reading debates: Evidence from science, art and ideology. *Teachers College Record, 94*, 315-328.

Chall, J. S. (1995). Ahead to the Greeks. *Issues in Education: Contributions From Educational Psychology, 1*, 83-85.

Chall, J. S. (1996). *Learning to read: The great debate* (3rd ed.). New York: McGraw-Hill.

Chall, J. S., & Popp, H. M. (1996). *Teaching and assessing phonics: A guide for teachers*. Cambridge, MA: Educator's Publishing Service.

Chomsky, N., & Halle, M. (1968). *The sound pattern of English*. New York: Harper & Row.

Claiborne, R. (1983). *Our marvelous native tongue: The life and times of the English language*. New York: Times Books.

Clay, M. M. (1991). *Becoming literate: The construction of inner control*. Portsmouth, NH: Heinemann.

Clay, M. M. (1993). *Reading Recovery: A guidebook for teachers in training*. Portsmouth, NH: Heinemann.

Consortium on Reading Excellence. (1999a). *CORE phonics survey*. Novato, CA: Arena.

Consortium on Reading Excellence. (1999b). *CORE reading research anthology*. Novato, CA: Arena.

Consortium on Reading Excellence. (2000).*CORE assessing reading: Multiple measures for kindergarten through eighth grade*. Novato, CA: Arena.

Crystal, D. (1995). *The Cambridge encyclopedia of the English language*. New York: Cambridge University Press.

Cunningham, A. (1990). Explicit versus implicit instruction in phonemic awareness. *Journal of Experimental Child Psychology, 50*, 429-444.

Cunningham, A., & Stanovich, K. E. (1993). Children's literacy environments and early word recognition subskills. *Reading and Writing: An Interdisciplinary Journal, 5*, 193-204.

Cunningham, A. E., & Stanovich, K. E. (1998). What reading does for the mind. *American Educator, 22*, 8-15.

Delpit, L. D. (1995). *Other people's children*. New York: New Press.

Depree, H., & Iversen S. (1994). *Early literacy in the classroom: A new standard for young readers*. Bothell, WA: The Wright Group.

Dickinson, D. K. (Ed.). (1994). *Bridges to literacy: Children, families, and schools*. Cambridge, MA: Blackwell.

Dickson, S. V., Collins, V. L., Simmons, D. C., & Kameenui, E. J. (1998). Metacognitive strategies: Research bases. In D. C. Simmons and E. J.

Kameenui (Eds.), *What reading research tells us about children with diverse learning needs: Bases and basics.* Mahwah, NJ: Erlbaum.

Dickson, S. V., Simmons, D. C., & Kameenui, E. J. (1998). Text organization: Research bases. In D. C. Simmons and E. J. Kameenui (Eds.),*What reading research tells us about children with diverse learning needs: Bases and basics.* Mahwah, NJ: Erlbaum.

Dolch, E. W. (1955). *Methods in reading.* Champaign, IL: Garrard.

Dowhower, S. L. (1987). Effects of repeated reading on second-grade transitional readers' fluency and comprehension. *Reading Research Quarterly, 22,* 389-406.

Dowhower, S. L. (1991). Speaking of prosody: Fluency's unattended bedfellow. *Theory Into Practice, 30*(3).

Ehri, L. C. (1992). Reconceptualizing the development of sight word reading and its relationship to recoding. In P. B. Gough, L. C. Ehri, & R. Treiman (Eds.), *Reading acquisition.* Mahwah, NJ: Erlbaum.

Ehri, L. C. (1994). Development of the ability to read words. In R. Ruddell & H. Singer (Eds.), *Theoretical models and processes of reading* (4th ed.), (pp. 323-358). Newark, DE: International Reading Association.

Ehri, L. C. (1995). Phases of development in reading words. *Journal of Research in Reading, 18,* 116-125.

Ehri, L. C., & McCormick, S. (1998). Phases of word learning: Implications for instruction with delayed and disabled readers. *Reading and Writing Quarterly, 14,* 135-63.

Foorman, B. R. (1995). Research on "The great debate over whole-language approaches to reading instruction." *School Psychology Review, 24,* 376-392.

Foorman, B. R. (1997). Why direct spelling instruction is important. *Scholastic Spelling Research Paper,* Vol. 2. New York: Scholastic.

Foorman, B. R., Francis, D. J., Fletcher, J. M., Schatschneider, C., & Mehta, P. (1998). The role of instruction in learning to read: Preventing reading failure in at-risk children. *Journal of Educational Psychology, 90*(1), 37-55.

Foorman, B. R., Francis, D. J., Shaywitz, S. E., Shaywitz, B. A., & Fletcher, J. M. (1997). The case for early reading intervention. In B. A. Blachman (Ed.), *Foundations of reading acquisition and dyslexia: Implications for early intervention.* Mahwah, NJ: Erlbaum.

Fry, E. (1994). *1000 instant words.* Westminster, CA: Teacher Created Materials.

Fry, E., Fountoukidis, D., & Polk, J. (1995). *The new reading teacher's book of lists.* Upper Saddle River, NJ: Prentice Hall.

Gallagher, M., & Pearson, P. D. (1989). Discussion, comprehension, and knowledge acquisition in content-area classrooms. *Technical Report #480.* Urbana-Champaign, IL: Center for the Study of Reading.

Ganske, K. (1996). *In other words: A resource of word lists for phonics, spelling, and vocabulary study.* Charlottesville: University of Virginia.

Gaskins, I., Ehri, L., Cress, C., O'Hara, C., & Donnelly, K. (1996). Procedures for word learning: Making discoveries about words. *The Reading Teacher, 50*(4), 312-327.

Gentry, J. R. (1998). *Five questions teachers ask about spelling (Zaner-Bloser Spelling Research Series)*. Columbus, OH: Zaner-Bloser.

Gillet, J. W., & Temple, C. (1994). *Understanding reading problems: Assessment and instruction* (4th ed.). New York: HarperCollins.

Goatley, V. J., Brock, C. H., & Raphael, T. E. (1995). Diverse learners participating in regular education "book clubs." *Reading Research Quarterly, 30*(3), 352-380.

Golick, M. (1987). *Playing With Words*. Markham, Ontario: Pembroke.

Golick, M. (1995). *Wacky Word Games*. Markham, Ontario: Pembroke.

Gough, P. B., & Walsh, M. A. (1991). Chinese, Phoenicians, and the graphic cipher of English. In S. A. Brady & D. P. Shankweiler (Eds.), *Phonological process in literacy: A tribute to Isabelle Y. Liberman*. Mahwah, NJ: Erlbaum.

Graves, D. (1994). *A fresh look at writing*. Portsmouth, NH: Heinemann.

Graves, M. F., Juel, C., & Graves, B. B. (1998). *Teaching reading in the twenty-first century*. Needham Heights, MA: Allyn & Bacon.

Griffith, P., & Olson, M. (1992). Phonemic awareness helps beginning readers break the code. *The Reading Teacher, 45*, 516-523.

Gross-Glenn, K., Jallad, B., Novoa, L., Helgren-Lempeses, V., & Lubs, H. A. (1990). *Reading & Writing, 2*, 161-173.

Hall, D. P., Cunningham, P. M., & Cunningham, J. W. (1995). Multilevel spelling instruction in third grade classrooms. In K. A. Hinchman, D. L. Leu, & C. Kinzer (Eds.), *Perspectives on literacy research and practice*. Chicago: National Reading Conference.

Hall, S. L., & Moats, L. C. (1999). *Straight talk about reading: How parents can make a difference during the early years*. Lincolnwood, IL: NTC/Contemporary Publishing Group.

Hanna, P. R., Hanna, J. S., Hodges, R. E., & Rudorf, E. H., Jr. (1966). *Phoneme-grapheme correspondences as cues to spelling improvement*. Washington, DC: U.S. Office of Education.

Harris, K. R., & Graham, S. (1996). Memo to constructivists: Skills count, too. *Educational Leadership, 53*, 26-29.

Hasbrouck, J. E., & Tindal, G. (1992). Curriculum-based oral reading fluency norms for students in grades 2 through 5. *Teaching Exceptional Children* (Spring), 41-44.

Henderson, E. H. (1981). *Learning to read and spell: The child's knowledge of words*. DeKalb, IL: Northern Illinois University Press.

Henderson, E. H., & Templeton, S. (1986). The development of spelling ability through alphabet, pattern, and meaning. *Elementary School Journal, 86*, 305-316.

Henry, M. C., Calfee, R., & La Salle, R. A. (1989). A structural approach to decoding and spelling. In S. McCormick & J. Zutell (Eds.), *Cognitive and social perspectives for literacy research and instruction: Thirty-eighth year-book of the National Reading Conference* (pp. 155 et seq.). National Reading Conference.

Honig, B., Diamond, L., & Gutlohn, L. (2000). *CORE teaching reading sourcebook for kindergarten through eighth grade.* Novato, CA: Arena Press.

Hoorn, J. V., Nourot, P. M., & Scales, B. (1993). *Play at the center of the curriculum.* New York: Macmillan.

Hughes, M., & Searle, D. (1996). Joe and Elly: Sight-based and sound-based approaches to literacy. *Whole Language Umbrella: Talking Points, 7*(4), 8-11.

Invernizzi, M., Abouzeid, M., & Gill, T. (1994). Using students' invented spelling as a guide for spelling instruction that emphasizes word study. *Elementary School Journal, 95*(2), 155-167.

Irvin, J. L. (1998). *Reading and the middle school student: Strategies to enhance literacy* (2nd ed.). Needham Heights, MA: Allyn & Bacon.

Jewel, T. A., & Pratt, D. (1999). Literature discussion in the primary grades: Children's thoughtful discourse about books and what teachers can do to make it happen. *The Reading Teacher, 52*(8), 842-850.

Juel, C. (1988). Learning to read and write: A longitudinal study of 54 children from first through fourth grades. *Journal of Educational Psychology, 80,* 437-447.

Juel, C. (1994). *Learning to read and write in one elementary school.* New York: Springer-Verlag.

Kameenui, E. J., Dixon, W., & Carnine, D. (1987). Issues in the design of vocabulary instruction. In M. G. McKeown & M. E. Curtis (Eds.), *The nature of vocabulary acquisition.* Mahwah, NJ: Erlbaum.

Kolers, P. (1976). Buswell's discoveries. In R. A. Monty & J. W. Senders (Eds.), *Eye movements and psychological processes.* Mahwah, NJ: Erlbaum.

Krashen, S. (1993). *The power of reading: Insights from the research.* Englewood, CO: Libraries Unlimited.

Langer, J. A. (1992). Rethinking literature instruction. In J. A. Langer (Ed.), *Literature instruction: A focus on student response* (pp. 35-53). Urbana, IL: National Council of Teachers of English.

Langer, J. A. (1993). Discussion as exploration: Literature and the horizon of possibilities. In G. E. Newell & R. K. Durst (Eds.), *Exploring texts: The role of discussion and writing in the teaching of literature* (pp. 23-43). Norwood, MA: Christopher-Gordon.

Langer, J. A. (1994). Focus on research: A response-based approach to reading literature. *Language Arts, 71,* 203-211.

Levin, J. R. (1993). Mnemonic strategies in the classroom: A twenty-year report card. *Elementary School Journal, 94,* 235-244.

Liberman, I. Y., Shankweiler, D., & Liberman, A. M. (1991). The alphabetic principle and learning to read. In *Phonology and reading disability: Solving the reading puzzle.* Washington, DC: International Academy for Research in

Learning Disabilities, Monograph Series, U.S. Department of Health and Human Services, Public Health Service; National Institutes of Health.

Lindamood, C. H., & Lindamood, P. C. (1984). *Auditory discrimination in depth*. Boston: Teaching Resources Corporation.

Lindamood, P. C., Bell, N., & Lindamood, C. (1992). Issues in phonological awareness assessment. *Annals of Dyslexia, 42*, 242-259.

Lovett, M. W. (1987). A developmental approach to reading disability: Accuracy and speed criteria of normal and deficient reading skill. *Child Development, 58*.

Lundberg, L. (1991). Phonemic awareness can be developed without reading processes. In *Literacy: A tribute to Isabelle Y. Liberman* (pp. 47-53). Hillsdale, NJ: Lawrence Erlbaum.

Lyon, G. R. (1994). *Research in learning disabilities at the NICHD*. Bethesda, MD: NICHD Technical Document/Human Learning and Behavior Branch.

Lyon, G. R. (1995). Research initiatives in learning disabilities: Contributions from scientists supported by the National Institute of Child Health and Human Development. *Journal of Child Neurology, 10*, 120-128.

Lyon, G. R. (1998, April 28). Statement of Dr. G. Reid Lyon Before the Committee on Labor and Human Resources, Washington, DC.

Mastropieri, M. A., Scruggs, T. E., & Fulk, B. J. (1990). Teaching abstract vocabulary with the keyword method: Effects on recall and comprehension. *Journal of Learning Disabilities, 23*, 92-107.

McCrum, R., Cran, W., & MacNeil, R. (1986). *The story of English*. New York: Viking Penguin.

McKeown, M. G., & Curtis, M. E. (Eds.). (1987). *The nature of vocabulary acquisition*. Hillsdale, NJ: Lawrence Erlbaum.

Mewhort, D. J. K., & Campbell, A. J. (1981). Toward a model of skilled reading: An analysis of performance in tachistoscopic tasks. In G. E. Mackinnon & T. G. Walker (Eds.), *Reading research: Advances in theory and practice* (pp. 39-118). New York: Academic Press.

Moats, L. C. (1994). The missing foundation in teacher education: Knowledge of the structure of spoken and written language. *Annals of Dyslexia, 44*, 157-168.

Moats, L. C. (1995). *Spelling: Development, disability, and instruction*. Timonium, MD: York Press.

Moats, L. C. (1999, June). *Teaching reading IS rocket science: What expert teachers of reading should know and be able to do*. Paper prepared for the American Federation of Teachers.

Moran, C., & Calfee, R. C. (1993). Comprehending orthography; Social construction of letter-sound in monolingual and bilingual programs. *Reading and Writing: An Interdisciplinary Journal, 5*, 205-225.

Morgan, J. N., & Willows, D. (1998). *Reducing the risk of literacy failure: Direct instruction in phonemic awareness and alphabetic coding for young ESL children.* Toronto: The University of Toronto, Department of Curriculum, OISE.

Morrow, L. M. (1986). Effects of story retelling on children's dictation of original stories. *Journal of Reading Behavior, 18,* 135-152.

Nagy, W. E. (1988). *Teaching vocabulary to improve reading comprehension.* Newark, DE: International Reading Association.

Nagy, W., & Anderson, R. C. (1984). How many words are there in printed school English? *Reading Research Quarterly, 19,* 304-330.

National Reading Panel. (2000). *Teaching children to read: An evidence-based assessment of the scientific research literature on reading and its implications for reading instruction.* Washington, DC: NICHD.

Ogle, D. M. (1986). K-W-L: A teaching model that develops active reading of expository text. *The Reading Teacher, 38*(6), 564-570.

O'Shea, L. J., Sindelar, P. T., & O'Shea, D. J. (1985). The effects of repeated readings and attentional cues on reading fluency and comprehension. *Journal of Reading Behavior, 17,* 129-142.

Pearson, D. P. (1993). Focus on research: Teaching and learning reading: A research perspective. *Language Arts, 70,* 502-511.

Pearson, P. D., Roehler, L. R., Dole, J. A., & Duffy, G. G. (1992). Developing expertise in reading comprehension. In S. J. Samuels and E. E. Farstrup (Eds.), *What research has to say about reading instruction.* Newark, DE: International Reading Association.

Peters, M. (1985). *Spelling: Caught or taught?* New York: Routledge.

Phenix, J. (1996). *The spelling teacher's book of lists.* Markham, Ontario: Pembroke.

Pinker, S. (1994). *The language instinct: How the mind creates language.* New York: HarperPerennial.

Pinnell, G. S., Pikulski, J. J., Wixson, K. K., Campbell, J. R., Gough, P. B., & Beatty, A. S. (1995). *Listening to children read aloud: Data from NAEP's Integrated Reading Performance Record (IRPR) at Grade 4* (NCES 95-726). Washington, DC: National Center for Education Statistics.

Pressley, M., & Cariglia-Bull, T. (1995). Decoding and the beginnings of reading. In M. Pressley & V. Woloshyn (Eds.), *Cognitive strategy instruction that really improves children's academic performance* (2nd ed., pp.19-56). Cambridge, MA: Brookline.

Pressley, M., El-Dinary, P. B., Gaskins, I., Schuder, T., Bergman, J. C., Almasi, J. & Brown, R. (1992). Beyond direct explanation: Transformational treatment of reading comprehension strategies. *Elementary School Journal, 92,* 513-556.

Pressley, M., Johnson, C. J., Symons, S., McGoldrick, J. S., & Kurita, J. A. (1989). Strategies that improve children's memory and comprehension of text. *Elementary School Journal, 90,* 3-32.

Pressley, M., & Lysynchuk, L. (1995). Vocabulary. In M. Pressley & V. Woloshyn (Eds.), *Cognitive strategy instruction that* really *improves children's academic performance* (2nd ed., pp. 101-115). Cambridge, MA: Brookline.

Pressley, M., & Rankin, J. (1994). More about whole language methods of reading instruction for students at risk for early reading failure. *Learning Disabilities Research & Practice, 9,* 157-168.

Pressley, M., Rankin, J., & Yokoi, L. (1996). A survey of instructional practices of primary teachers nominated as effective in promoting literacy. *Elementary School Journal, 96,* 363-384.

Pressley, M., Symons, S., McGoldrick, J. A., & Snyder, B. L. (1995). Reading comprehension strategies. In M. Pressley & V. Woloshyn (Eds.), *Cognitive strategy instruction that* really *improves children's academic performance* (2nd ed., pp. 57-100). Cambridge, MA: Brookline Books.

Pressley, M., & Woloshyn, V. (1995). *Cognitive strategy instruction that* really *improves children's academic performance* (2nd ed.). Cambridge, MA: Brookline Books.

Raphael, T. (1994) Book club: An alternative framework for reading instruction. *The Reading Teacher, 48,* 102-116.

Raphael, T., & Goatley, V. J. (1994). The teacher as "More Knowledgeable Other." National Reading Conference Yearbook, Proceedings, 1994.

Raphael, T., Goatley, V., McMahon, S., & Woodman, D. (1995). Teaching literacy through student book clubs: Promoting meaningful conversations about books. In N. Roser & M. Martinez (Eds.), *Supporting children's responses to literature: Book talk and beyond.* Newark, DE: International Reading Association.

Raphael, T. E. (1982). Question-answering strategies for children. *The Reading Teacher, 36,* 186-190.

Rosenshine, B., & Meister, C. (1994). Reciprocal teaching: A review of the research. *Review of Educational Research, 64,* 479-530.

Samuels, S. J. (1979). The method of repeated reading. *The Reading Teacher, 32,* 403-408.

Samway, K. D., & & Whang, G. (1996). *Literature study circles in a multicultural classroom.* York, ME: Stenhouse.

Schwartz, R. M., & Raphael, T. E. (1985). Concept of definition: A key to improving students' vocabulary. *The Reading Teacher, 39,* 198-203.

Scott, J. A., Hiebert, E. H., & Anderson, R. C. (1994). Research as we approach the millennium: Beyond "Becoming a Nation of Readers." In F. Lehr & J. Osborn (Eds.), *Reading, language, and literacy: Instruction for the twenty-first century* (pp. 253-280). Hillsdale, NJ: Lawrence Erlbaum.

Shany, M. T., & Biemiller, A. (1995). Assisted reading practice: Effects on performance for poor readers in Grades 3 & 4. *Reading Research Quarterly, 50*(3), 382-395.

Share, D. L. (1995). Phonological recoding and self-teaching: Sine qua non of reading acquisition. *Cognition: International Journal of Cognitive Science, 55,* 151-218.

Share, D. L., & Stanovich, K. E. (1995a). Accommodating individual differences in critiques: Replies to our commentators. *Issues in Education: Contributions From Educational Psychology, 1,*105-121.

Share, D. L., & Stanovich, K. E. (1995b). Cognitive processes in early reading development: Accommodating individual differences into a mode of acquisition. *Issues in Education: Contributions From Educational Psychology, 1,* 1-57.

Shaywitz, S. E. (1996). Dyslexia. *Scientific American, 275.*

Short, K. G., & Klassen, C. (1993). Literature circles: Hearing children's voices. In B. E. Cullinan (Ed.), *Children's voices: Talk in the classroom.* Newark, DE: International Reading Association.

Shu, H., Anderson, R., & Shang, H. (1995). Incidental learning of word meanings while reading. *Reading Research Quarterly, 30,* 76-86.

Slavin, R. E., Madden, N. A., Dolan, L. J., & Wasik, B. A. (1996). *Every child, every school: Success for all.* Thousand Oaks, CA: Corwin.

Smith, F. S. (1982). *Understanding reading* (3rd ed.). New York: Holt, Rinehart & Winston.

Snow, C. E., Burns, M. S., & Griffin, P. (1998). *Preventing reading difficulties in young children.* Washington, DC: National Academy Press.

Stahl, S. A. (1992). Saying the "p" word: Nine guidelines for exemplary phonics instruction. *The Reading Teacher, 45,* 618-625.

Stahl, S. A. (1999). *Vocabulary development.* Cambridge, MA: Brookline Books.

Stahl, S. A., & Kapinus, B. A. (1991). Possible sentences: Predicting word meanings to teach content area vocabulary. *The Reading Teacher, 45,* 36-38.

Stanovich, K. E. (1986). Matthew effects in reading: Some consequences of individual differences in the acquisition of literacy. *Reading Research Quarterly, 21,* 360-407.

Stanovich, K. E. (1993a). Does reading make you smarter? Literacy and the development of verbal intelligence. In H. Reese (Ed.), *Advances in child development and behavior* (Vol. 25, pp. 133-180). San Diego, CA: Academic Press.

Stanovich, K. E. (1993b). Romance and reality. *The Reading Teacher, 47,* 280-291.

Stauffer, R. G. (1975). *Directing the reading-thinking process.* New York: Harper & Row.

Stein, M., Johnson, B., & Gutlohn, L. (1999). Analyzing beginning reading programs: The relationship between decoding instruction and text. *Remedial and Special Education, 20,* 275-287.

Taylor, D. S. (1981). English spelling: A help rather than a hindrance. *English Language Teaching Journal, 35,* 316-321.

Tierney, R. J. (1982). Essential considerations for developing basic reading comprehension skills. *School Psychology Review II(3)*, 299-305.

Torgesen, J. K. (1995). Instruction for reading disabled children: Questions about knowledge into practice. *Issues in Education: Contributions From Educational Psychology, 1*, 91-95.

Torgesen, J. K. (1997). The prevention and remediation of reading disabilities: Evaluating what we know from research. *Journal of Academic Language Therapy, 1*, 11-47.

Torgesen, J. K., & Barker, T. A. (1995). Computers as aids in the prevention and remediation of reading disabilities. *Learning Disabilities Quarterly, 18*, 76-87.

Torgesen, J. K., & Bryant, B. R. (1994). *Phonological awareness training for reading*. Austin, TX: PRO-ED.

Torgesen, J. K., & Hecht, S. A. (1996). Preventing and remediating reading disabilities: Instructional variables that make a difference for special students. In M. F. Graves, B. M. Taylor, & P. van den Broek (Eds.), *The first R: Every child's right to read*. Cambridge: MIT Press.

Torgesen, J. K., Wagner, R, K., & Rashotte, C. A. (1994). Longitudinal studies of phonological processing and reading, *Journal of Learning Disabilities, 27*, 276-286.

Trachtenberg, P., & Ferrugia, A. (1989). Big books from little voices: Reaching high-risk beginning readers. *The Reading Teacher, 42*, 284-289.

Treiman, R. (1996). *Why spelling? The benefits of incorporating spelling into beginning reading instruction*. Paper presented at the Conference on Word Recognition in Beginning Literacy, College Park, MD.

Treiman, R., & Baron, J. (1981). Segmental analysis ability: Development and relation to reading ability. In G. E. MacKinnon and T. G. Waller (Eds.), *Reading research: Advances in theory and practice*. (Vol. 3.) New York: Academic Press.

Tunmer, W. E., & Chapman, J. W. (1995). Context use in early reading development: Premature exclusion of a source of individual differences? *Issues in Education: Contributions From Educational Psychology, 1*, 97-100.

Vellutino, F. R., Scanlon, D. M., Sipay, E., Small, S., Pratt, A., Chen, R., & Denckla, M. (1996). Cognitive profiles of difficult-to-remediate and readily remediated poor readers: Early intervention as a vehicle for distinguishing between cognitive and experiential deficits as basic causes of specific reading disability. *Journal of Educational Psychology, 88*, 601-638.

Venezky, R. L. (1970). *The structure of English orthography*. The Hague: Mouton.

Watts, S., & Graves, M. (1995). *Fostering word consciousness*. Unpublished manuscript.

Wharton-McDonald, R., & Pressley, M. (1998). Literacy instruction in nine first-grade classrooms: Teacher characteristics and student achievement. *Elementary School Journal, 99*, 101-139.

White, T. G., Slater, W. H., & Graves, M. E. (1989). Yes/No method of vocabulary assessment: Valid for whom and useful for what? *Cognitive and social perspectives for literacy research and instruction.* Chicago: National Reading Conference.

Woloshyn, V., & Pressley, M. (1995). Spelling. In M. Pressley & V. Woloshyn (Eds.), *Cognitive strategy instruction that* really *improves children's academic performance* (2nd ed., pp. 116-152). Cambridge, MA: Brookline Books.

Wood, E., Woloshyn, V. E., & Willoughby, T. (1995). *Cognitive strategy instruction for middle and high schools.* Cambridge, MA: Brookline Books.

Wylie, R., & Durrell, D. (1970). Teaching vowels through phonograms. *Elementary English, 47.*

Yopp, H. K. (1992). Developing phonemic awareness in young children. *The Reading Teacher, 45,* 696-703.

Young, S. (1994) *The Scholastic rhyming dictionary.* New York: Scholastic.

Zutell, J. (1998). *A student-active learning approach to spelling instruction.* Zaner-Bloser Spelling Research Series. Columbus, OH: Zaner-Bloser.

Suggested Reading

Baker, S., Simmons, D. C., & Kameenui, E. J. (1998). Vocabulary acquisition: Instructional and curricular basics and implications. In D. C. Simmons & E. J. Kameenui (Eds.), *What reading research tells us about children with diverse learning needs. Bases and basics.* Mahwah, NJ: Erlbaum.

Bear, D. (1982). *Patterns of oral reading across stages of word knowledge.* Unpublished doctoral dissertation, University of Virginia, Charlottesville, VA.

Bowey, J. (1995). On the contribution of phonological sensitivity to phonological recoding. *Issues in Education, 1,* 65-69.

Brown, R., Pressley, M., Schuder, T., & Van Meter, P. (1994). *A quasi-experimental validation of transactional strategies instruction with previously low-achieving grade-2 readers.* College Park: University of Maryland, National Reading Research Center.

Calfee, R. C. (1995). A behind-the-scenes look at reading acquisition. *Issues in Education, 1,* 77-82.

California Reading Task Force. (1995). *Every child a reader.* Sacramento: California Department of Education.

Center, Y., Wheldall, K., Freeman, L., Outhred, L., & McNaught, M. (1995). An evaluation of Reading Recovery. *Reading Research Quarterly, 30,* 240-260.

Hiebert, E. H. (1994). Reading Recovery in the United States: What difference does it make to an age cohort? *Educational Researcher, 23*(9), 15-25.

Hiebert, E. H., & Taylor, B. M. (Eds.). (1994). *Getting reading right from the start: Effective early literacy intervention.* Boston: Allyn & Bacon.

Iversen, S., & Tunmer, W. E. (1993). Phonological processing skills and the Reading Recovery Program, *Journal of Educational Psychology, 85,* 112-120.

Johnson, T. D., & Louis, D. R. (1990). *Bringing it all together: A program for literacy.* Portsmouth, NH: Heinemann.

Knapp, M. S., Shields, P. M., & Turnbull, B. J. (1995). Academic challenge in high poverty classrooms. *Phi Delta Kappan, 76,* 770-776.

Lundberg, L. (1991). Phonemic awareness can be developed without reading processes. In *Literacy: A tribute to Isabelle Y. Liberman* (pp. 47-53). Hillsdale, NJ: Lawrence Erlbaum.

Lyons, C. A., & Beaver, J. (1995). Reducing retention and learning disability placement through Reading Recovery: An educationally sound cost-effective choice. In R. Allington & S. Walmsley (Eds.), *No quick fix: Rethinking literacy programs in America's elementary schools* (pp. 116-136). New York: Teachers College Press.

McPike, E. (1995). Learning to read: Schooling's first mission. *American Educator, 19,* 12-15.

Nagy, W. E. (1995, April). *What do we know about vocabulary? Toward a state-of-the-art.* Panel presentation and interactive symposium at the American Educational Research Association, San Francisco.

Pinnell, G. S., DeFord, D. E., Lyons, C. A., & Bryk, A. (1995). Response to Rasinski. *Reading Research Quarterly, 30,* 272-275.

Pinnell, G. S., Lyons, C. A., DeFord, D. E., Bryk, A. S., & Seltzer, M. (1994). Comparing instructional models for the literacy education of high risk first graders. *Reading Research Quarterly, 29,* 8-39.

Pressley, M., El-Dinary, P. B., Gaskins, I., Schuder, T., Bergman, J. C., Almasi, J., & Brown, R. (1992). Beyond direct explanation: Transformational treatment of reading comprehension strategies. *Elementary School Journal, 92,* 513-556.

Rasinski, T. (1995a). On the effects of Reading Recovery: A response to Pinnell, Lyons, DeFord, Bryk, & Seltzer. *Reading Research Quarterly, 30,* 264-270.

Rasinski, T. (1995b). Reply to Pinnell, DeFord, Lyons, & Bryk. *Reading Research Quarterly, 30,* 276-277.

Rosenblatt, L. M. (1978). *The reader, the text, the poem: The transactional theory of the literary work.* Carbondale: Southern Illinois University Press.

Rosenblatt, L. M. (1983). *Literature as exploration.* New York: Modern Language Association. (Original work published in 1938)

Shefelbine, J. (1995). Learning and using phonics in beginning reading. *Scholastic Literacy Research Papers, 10.* New York: Scholastic.

Smith, F. S. (1992). Learning to read: The never-ending debate. *Phi Delta Kappan, 73,* 432-441.

Topping, K. J. (1995). Cued spelling: A powerful technique for parent and peer tutoring, *The Reading Teacher, 48*(5).

Williams, J. P. (1991). The meaning of a phonics base for reading instruction. In *All language and the creation of literacy* (pp. 9-19). Proceedings of the Orton Dyslexia Society Symposia, "Whole Language and Phonics" and "Literacy and Language." Baltimore: Orton Dyslexia Society.

Yopp, H. K. (1995). A test for assessing phonemic awareness in young children. *The Reading Teacher, 49,* 20-29.

Zutell, J. (1992). An integrated view of word knowledge: Correctional studies of the relationships among spelling, reading, and conceptual development. In S. Templeton & D. Bear (Eds.), *Development of orthographic knowledge and the foundations of literacy: A memorial festschrift for Edmund Henderson.* Mahwah, NJ: Erlbaum.

Index